Common Worship Considered

by Peter Toon and Louis R. Tarsitano

Neither Archaic nor Obsolete:
the Language of Common Prayer and Public Worship

COMMON WORSHIP CONSIDERED

A Liturgical Journey Examined

by

PETER TOON

Edgeways

copyright © 2003 The Brynmill Press Ltd

first published in 2003 by Edgeways Books
a division of The Brynmill Press Ltd
Pockthorpe Cottage
Denton, Harleston, Norfolk. IP20 0AS England

typeset by the Publishers and printed in England by
Antony Rowe Ltd
Bumper's Farm Industrial Estate
Chippenham Wiltshire SN14 6LH

ISBN 0 907839 78 9

British Library Cataloguing in Publication Data: a catalogue record of this book
is available from the British Library.

The right of Peter Toon to be identified as the author of this work has been
asserted by him in accordance with the Copyright, Designs and Patents Act
1988.

All Brynmill publications are unsubsidized.

www.edgewaysbooks.com

Contents

Gracious Father, I humbly beseech Thee for Thy Holy Catholic Church. Fill it with all truth, in all truth, with peace. Where it is corrupt, purge it. Where it is in error, direct it. Where it is superstitious, rectify it. Where anything is amiss, reform it. Where it is right, strengthen and confirm it. Where it is in want, furnish it. Where it is divided and rent asunder, make up the breaches of it, O Thou Holy One of Israel.

William Laud, Works, Library of Anglo-Catholic Theology III, p. 67

Preface

In the period before I left the Church of England in 1990 to work in the Episcopal Church of the United States of America, I used both *The Book of Common Prayer* (1662)[1] and *The Alternative Service Book 1980*. When I returned to the Church of England in December 2001 it was to a parish which used the *Prayer Book* for Sunday services, and *Common Worship*, sometimes, for marriage and baptism. *Common Worship* is the set of forms of service, directories and pastoral aids, in progress, of which the main volume appeared in 2000.

On arrival in America I soon realised that the book with the title, *The Book of Common Prayer ... according to the use of The Episcopal Church* (1979) is not in fact the *Prayer Book* as I had known it in England. It is much more like *The Alternative Service Book 1980*. Within its covers most services are in "contemporary language" and a few in "traditional language". The latter are based upon, but not identical with, services in the real American Prayer Book, *The Book of Common Prayer* (1789, 1891 & 1928). It soon became apparent to me that the General Convention of the Episcopal Church had in 1979 effectively changed the meaning of "Common Prayer". While the Church of England in 1980 had carefully distinguished the *Prayer Book* from the new services, the Episcopal Church had in 1979 effectively laid the classical *Prayer Book* to rest and pirated its title and name for a new and different type of book. Since the 1970s the Prayer Book Society of the USA has been working hard to keep the 1928 *Prayer Book* in print and to support those parishes which still desire to use it.

In the decade or so that I worked in America, I watched the Episcopal Church produce, and the General Convention approve, a series of trial services which increasingly expressed as church doctrine the feminist agenda for the "non-exclusion" of women. What is referred to as "gender neutral language" was used both in referring to human beings and to God, even as the acceptance of the ordination of women was made part of the official "creed" of the Church. At the time that I returned to England, the Liturgical and Music Commission of the

1 Unless otherwise stated the *Prayer Book* means the 1662 *Book of Common Prayer*.

Episcopal Church was engaged in a major review of the liturgical needs of its membership in order to present a report to the General Convention in July 2003 as the basis for the production of a replacement for the 1979 Prayer Book by 2009. This is expected to be a multiple provision of services and outlines of services in various languages.

Having missed the English debates of the 1990s, in the General Synod and elsewhere, concerning new liturgy, I had to make up for lost time. Thus I began to study the provisions of *Common Worship*, and the books produced to explain this new liturgical phenomenon. There was much more to look at than I first expected! Happily, I found that my studies of new liturgy and my observation of change in the Episcopal Church of America were a great help to me in my evaluation of the texts of *Common Worship*. What began as a personal quest for understanding, is now offered to others for their perusal and examination.

The title, *Common Worship Considered*, accurately represents what I have been doing and what I believe are the contents of this book. The subtitle, which refers to a Journey, points to the image preferred by the Liturgical Commission to cover all their provisions from Baptism to Funeral.

The primary vantage point from which my consideration has been made is the high ground of the Formularies of the Church of England, since it is to them that the doctrine of all alternative services is to conform. My hope is that this small book helps others to engage in calm and rational consideration.

Perhaps I need to say that together with my friend, the Revd Dr Louis R. Tarsitano of Savannah, Georgia, I have written a short book which in many ways paves the way for this one. It concerns (a) the origins, nature, characteristics and use of the classic English idiom/dialect/language of public worship and common prayer; and (b) the efforts made from the 1960s to replace it with a new language of prayer, based upon the secular idiom of our day. Its full title is: *Neither Archaic nor Obsolete: The English Language of Common Prayer and Public Worship* (2003) and it is published by the same publisher as the present volume. I make some use of it in Chapter Ten. I hope that readers of this book will obtain and read the previous one.

I need to thank various persons for their help, particularly Ian Robinson, Louis Tarsitano, Roger Beckwith, Raymond Chapman, Prudence Dailey, Graham Eglington, Arthur Capey, George Westhaver, Colin Podmore and my wife, Vita Toon.

PETER TOON, The Rectory, Biddulph Moor ST8 7HP
Easter 2003

CHAPTER ONE

The Preface of Common Worship

In most cases the Preface of a book is written last of all. When it is for an important publication, such as an official Report of a government or a Prayer Book for a National Church, it is usually most informative, providing information not only about the contents but also about the general philosophy supporting them.

The Preface to *The Book of the Common Prayer* (1549) was written by Archbishop Thomas Cranmer after the work of creating this new prayer book in English had been completed. It makes claims about the reading of Holy Scripture in the ancient Church, the duty to read through the Bible every year and to pray the Psalms daily and the whole Psalter monthly; and these are given practical embodiment in the 1549 *Prayer Book* itself. This Preface also explains the four principles which guided the reform of the complex medieval services and their rubrics to produce the new ones with simplified directions. The principles are the purgation of unsuitable material, employment of the vernacular language, simplification of ritual, and uniformity of use in the nation. Finally, where there are doubtful cases the power of interpretation is to be given to the bishops.

In *The Book of Common Prayer* of 1662 Cranmer's Preface is renamed "Concerning the Service of the Church" and a new Preface written by Dr Sanderson, Bishop of Lincoln, takes pride of place. It sets forth the principles which had guided the Church of England in revising the *Prayer Book* from time to time, the circumstances that led to the revision of 1661, and the reasons for the chief alterations then introduced.

When the *Prayer Book* of 1662 was adapted in 1789 for use in the newly organized Protestant Episcopal Church of the United States of America, it contained a Preface written by Dr William Smith. This not only constitutes one of the monuments of eighteenth-century prose but also provides an important introduction to this first official *Book of Common Prayer* for an independent America. It summarizes the principles of worship as they are known in the Anglican way; it provides the reasons for the edition of an American *Prayer Book*; it describes the nature of the revised *Prayer Book* and ends with a warm commendation of this book to the membership of the Church.

In the case of Cranmer's, Sanderson's and Smith's prefaces, it would be possible to begin with the information supplied and the claims made and then test them by studying the contents of the 1549 & 1662 & 1789 Prayer Books. Here we shall perform a similar task and examine the Preface to *Common Worship: Services and Prayers for the Church of England* (2000), taking it paragraph by paragraph in order to be clear as to what is being claimed and affirmed. This careful examination will then point us into various forms of enquiry concerning the provision of services and prayers called *Common Worship*.

However, before we turn to the Preface it will be useful to have before us a bird's eye view of liturgical revision in the Church of England, which began about a century ago with the report of the Royal Commission on Ecclesiastical Discipline in 1906. From this began the preparation of what eventually (after being halted by World War I) became the 1928 *Prayer Book*. Though approved by the Church Assembly this revision of *The Book of Common Prayer* of 1662 was rejected by the House of Commons, because it made too many concessions to Anglo-Catholics for Protestants to be happy with it. After World War II, the first services to be authorised by the Church Assembly in 1964 were called "Series 1" and were in essence certain services from the 1928 *Prayer Book*. "Series 2" followed and though retaining the traditional idiom of prayer and addressing the "Thou-God", it did not begin from the 1662 text but rather from patristic models. Also it adopted the position of "studied ambiguity" of doctrinal expression (e. g., of the presence of Christ in the Eucharist) and this approach has remained part of the liturgical scene. In 1973 "Series 3" appeared and for the first time in official Church of England liturgy a "contemporary" idiom was used and God was addressed as the "You-God". Then in 1980 *The Alternative Service Book 1980: Services authorized for use in the Church of England in conjunction with the The Book of Common Prayer* was published, containing primarily versions of the experimental "Series 3" services of the last decade or more. The full title of this Prayer Book is significant, for the Worship and Doctrine Measure of 1974 had insisted that the Formularies of the Church of England were unchanged and thus *The Book of Common Prayer* was both the primary manual of worship and also a standard of doctrine (with the Articles of Religion and the Ordinal) of the established Church.

In 2000 *Common Worship* replaced *The Alternative Service Book 1980,* but not all the parts of it were published immediately. They were to appear over a period of several years. The former Liturgical Publishing Group (which was chaired by the Bishop of Guildford) was responsible for the publication of the first and main volume, containing Sunday services and the Baptism Service, and for the Preface. The Preface, however, reflected the views of the Liturgical Commission (which is chaired by the Bishop of Salisbury). This knowledge that several hands had a part in the creation of the Preface may make the more difficult our aim to gain from it as much clarity as possible concerning the specific purpose of and claims for *Common Worship.* Further, the involvement of several parties probably explains why, as we shall see, it does not always have coherence and why it appears to jump about from topic to topic. Nevertheless, in a roundabout way, this imperfection of style does perhaps provide more insight into what is being claimed for *Common Worship* than a more polished style would have done, such as there was in the Preface to *The Alternative Service Book 1980.*

1 Great Significance

The publication of Common Worship *is an occasion of great significance in the life of the Church of England, because the worship of God is central to the life of his Church.*

The appearance of the main volume with the sub-title, "Services and Prayers for the Church of England" in 2000, along with other volumes bearing the primary title of *Common Worship,* has certainly been a significant, open-ended event, which had a beginning but (at the time of writing in 2003) has not yet an end. The creation, approving, editing and publishing of such a great amount of material represent a major achievement. In comparison, the work involved in the making of the 1928 *Prayer Book,* Series 1, 2 and 3, and *The Alternative Service Book 1980,* seems minimal!

It is obvious (a) that the removal of *The Alternative Service Book* which had been in use since 1980 and the arrival of *Common Worship* have created a tremendous amount of work for individuals, commissions, committees, synods and the like, and (b) the adoption and reception in parishes have created great expense, disruption, opportunities and changes. We may admit that these facts alone merit the use of the adjective "great" as a descriptive term before "significance".

But the adjective "great" seems to be intended to point to a positive idea, for example, that of "the dawn of a new era" or "the arrival of new opportunities with fresh resources". In fact, the clause "because the worship of God is central to the life of the Church" seems to be related to "great significance" and suggests the positive idea that with the arrival of *Common Worship* the Church of England is able to worship God better than ever before.

Certainly no Christian can disagree with the claim that "the worship of God is central to the life of the Church". Yet he may enthusiastically embrace this affirmation while also having serious doubts that the provisions of *Common Worship* are the best way to provide for, or to experience, the centrality of worship in the Church of England.

It is interesting, if not worrying, that at the beginning of the twenty-first century the Church of England is doing the very opposite to what it did in the middle of the sixteenth century. At that time, for the worship of the whole nation, it reduced multiple, medieval volumes to one compact, modern book, *The Book of the Common Prayer* (1549). Now it is creating as the replacement for one book, *The Alternative Service Book 1980* a small library of new volumes under the general heading of *Common Worship*. To keep track of these new large or small books/booklets, and the various commentaries produced to explain them, is not easy, except for the specialist or the enthusiast. Those who possess *The Church of England Year Book, 2003,* can consult a full list on pages 229 and 330, although it is now out of date. While it is comparatively easy to remember and recite the list of medieval liturgical volumes (from the Missal through the Breviary to the Pontifical and Processional), the list of authorized services alternative to *The Book of Common Prayer* (1662) is so long as to demand an excessively fine memory.

2 *Worship and Identity*

The forms of worship authorized in the Church of England express our faith and help to create our identity. The Declaration of Assent is placed at the beginning of this volume to remind us of this. When ministers make the Declaration, they affirm their loyalty to the Church of England's inheritance of faith and accept their share in the responsibility to proclaim the faith "afresh in each generation".

Certainly the way in which the congregations in the cathedrals and parish churches of the land engage in worship each Sunday is a public expression of the faith of those who attend. It is true also that it creates an Anglican identity, one that differs from that, say, of the Salvation Army or the Roman Catholic Church. This Anglican identity was for centuries reasonably straightforward because intimately connected to *The Book of Common Prayer*, whether used and celebrated with little or much ceremonial. Since the arrival of trial services, Series 1, 2 and 3 and then *The Alternative Service Book 1980*, that identity has become less clear, if for no other reason than the general use in public worship of many different rites in two different idioms, "traditional" and "contemporary" language.

Obviously the clergy/ministers who lead the services of the Church of England have much to do with the public expression of faith and it is they (together with Readers and Lay Workers) who do much to establish an Anglican identity. With these persons most of this paragraph is specifically concerned.

The "Declaration of Assent" begins with a preface in which the Church of England is said to be a part of the one Church of God and to profess the Faith uniquely revealed in the Holy Scriptures and set forth in the Catholic Creeds. Her specific Formularies are *The Thirty-Nine Articles of Religion* (1562), *The Book of Common Prayer* (1662) and *The Ordinal* (1662)—all of which are usually bound together. So it is presumed that the expression of worship, doctrine, morality and discipline in *Common Worship* is based on the Bible and in harmony with that which is received from the authoritative Scriptures, and witnessed to in the Creeds and Formularies. The one and the same Faith, it is rightly claimed, is to be proclaimed afresh in and to each generation, but it is to be anchored in the Bible, the Creeds and the Formularies.

In the light of this information why does not the title page, as did the title page of the 1980 liturgy, state, "Services authorized for use in the Church of England in conjunction with The Book of Common Prayer" or something similar? Further, why are not *The Articles of Religion* and the Athanasian Creed printed somewhere in the collection of texts that is *Common Worship*?

3 Old and New together

Common Worship *draws together the rich inheritance of the past and the very best of our contemporary forms of worship. In this volume we bring together the services of* The Book of Common Prayer *as they are used today and newer liturgies in both traditional and contemporary style. The* Book of Common Prayer *remains the permanently authorized provision for public worship in the Church of England, whereas the newer liturgies are authorized until further resolution of the General Synod. This combination of old and new provides for the diverse worshipping needs of our communities, within an ordered structure which affirms our essential unity and common life.*

In this paragraph, we are presented with certain facts and several claims. The facts are (a) the permanent position of *The Book of Common Prayer* (1662) in the Church of England, guaranteed by Act of Parliament as both the primary Prayer Book and also the standard of doctrine; and (b) the temporary authorization of *Common Worship*, for as long as the General Synod permits.

Inside *Common Worship* are services from *The Book of Common Prayer* (1662)—specifically, Morning and Evening Prayer, the Litany and The Order for Holy Communion. Yet these services are not identical with their originals since they are printed "as they are used", that is, as they are used in general here and there in parishes of the Church of England. Further, "The Order for Holy Communion" is provided in this amended way without the Collects (Cranmer's jewelled miniatures) and the ancient Eucharistic Lectionary of the *Prayer Book*. Also the Lectionary to be used at the *Prayer Book* forms of Morning and Evening Prayer on Sundays is not one of those (of 1662, 1871 or 1922) authorized for use with the *Prayer Book* services.

Thus the (edited) services of the *Prayer Book*, which in their natural habitat do not know any competition, are here placed as one option amongst many, so that the user can choose as he pleases. With them are made available services which are amended forms of some of those that were in *The Alternative Service Book 1980* and others that have been produced since then. These are available in both "traditional" and "contemporary" language so that a parish may have a modern rite in the old language or an old rite in contemporary language.

This diversity provides multiple options, and such could seem to be a recipe for chaos, the very opposite of unity in Church life and worship. However, it is claimed that *"This combination of old and new provides for the diverse worshipping needs of our communities, within an ordered structure which affirms our essential unity and common life."* Apparently unity is preserved and common worship/prayer sustained because there is an "ordered structure". It is not clear whether the ordered structure is the provision of a List of the Contents or Ingredients of each Liturgy (its Shape), or a List of all the Rites, Services and Liturgies, or the Synodical Legislation that permits it all. Whatever precisely is the "essential unity" and "common life" arising from *Common Worship* they are certainly different in essence and ethos from the earlier expressions of these when only *The Book of Common Prayer* was authorized and in use from 1549 through to the 1960s.

4 *Engagement in Worship*

The services provided here are rich and varied. This reflects the multiplicity of contexts in which worship is offered today. They encourage an imaginative engagement in worship, opening the way for people in the varied circumstances of their lives to experience the love of God in Jesus Christ in the life and power of the Holy Spirit. In the worship of God the full meaning and beauty of our humanity is consummated and our lives are opened to the promise God makes for all creation—to transform and renew it in love and goodness.

Here several claims are made and a theology of worship is briefly stated.

One claim is that the services are "rich and varied". There can be no quarrel with the claim of "variety" for such is obvious even to a cursory glance at the provisions of services. Whether they are "rich" depends upon how one evaluates their individual ingredients and style as well as the total impact of their contents.

Another claim is that each and all of them, those in traditional and those in contemporary language "encourage an imaginative engagement in worship". It is difficult to see why the imagination is particularly singled out, and not, say, human reason. Human beings are so different and thus some are drawn into worship through the kindling of their emotions and affections, some through their imagination, some through the contemplation of their minds and some through the determination of their wills. The Holy Ghost works in multiple ways to lead people into a relation with the Father through the Lord Jesus Christ.

The theology of worship expressed here seems at first sight to be pointing to the beatific vision of the age to come, but is in fact, on closer examination, referring to something less, some experience attainable in this life through the use of *Common Worship* services. It may be observed that for orthodox theology the "full meaning and beauty of our humanity" is only seen and known in the perfected humanity of the Incarnate Son of God, the Lord Jesus, through, by and in whom the faithful approach the Father of glory in adoration and praise. Thus only as sanctified and redeemed by him and in union with him can sinful human beings begin to see the beauty of our humanity as it is displayed in the One who is the new Adam, even Jesus the Christ. It would appear that here an attempt is being made to relate a theology of creation (which has been a popular theme in recent times) to a theology of worship, and because compressed into a few words, the meaning is not clear. It is certainly not an expression of the theology of the *Prayer Book* or of the Articles of Religion. This is because it seems to be making positive assertions about the future of the present sinful world/creation which run contrary to the traditional doctrine of the judgement and the passing away of the present world and the arrival of "the new creation" of "the new heavens and the new earth".

5 *Jesus Christ and Challenge*

The publication of these services is a challenge to us. It is a challenge to worship God better and to take the greatest care in preparing and celebrating worship. It is a challenge to draw the whole community of the people we serve into the worship of God. Central to our worship is the proclamation of the one, perfect self-offering of the Son to the Father. The Gospel of Jesus Christ is at the heart of Common Worship.

Here we learn that the arrival of *Common Worship* in the parish church presents two specific challenges, which may be called noble aims. The first is to improve the way in which parishes have engaged in worship—to worship God better; and the second is to make the services so attractive that they draw, as a magnet of grace, the local people into the worship of God. (The word "community" is not used in the *Prayer Book* or the King James Version but is much used in modern church talk. Here it seems to mean those outside the fellowship of the local church. Previously "communities"[1] may refer to the people within the geographical parish or to the people who actually attend worship. In paragraph 6 "the gathering of the community" is apparently the assembly of the church members for worship.)

Having stated the challenges or noble aims of contemporary worship, the Preface makes another statement of a theology of worship. It is affirmed that central to worship is "the proclamation of the one, perfect self-offering of the Son to the Father", and this is then equated with "the Gospel of Jesus Christ". By this is presumably meant the total life, ministry, death on the Cross, burial and descent into Hades, the Resurrection and Exaltation, and the Session at the Father's right hand of Jesus, the Messiah and Lord. It is the self-offering of the Incarnate Son to the Father in the eternal Spirit and is made in his capacity as the new Adam, the Messiah, the Mediator, the Prophet, Priest and King. Without this self-offering there is no salvation for Jew or Gentile. Whether in fact this Gospel is at the heart of all the services of *Common Worship*, as claimed here, can only be known through a most careful examination of the content of the many, varied services, rites and prayers, some of which have yet to appear.

1 Paragraph 3

6 *The Worship of Pilgrims*

Those who make the Declaration of Assent are charged with bringing the grace and truth of Christ to this generation and making him known to those in their care. Worship not only strengthens Christians for witness and service, but is itself a forum in which Christ is made known. Worship is for the whole people of God, who are fellow pilgrims on a journey of faith, and those who attend services are all at different stages of that journey. Indeed worship itself is a pilgrimage—a journey into the heart of the love of God. A number of the services themselves—particularly that of Holy Baptism— are celebrated in stages. In each case the journey through the liturgy has a clear structure with signposts for those less familiar with the way. It moves from the gathering of the community through the liturgy of the Word to an opportunity of transformation, sacramental or non-sacramental, after which those present are sent out to put their faith into practice.

Once again a reference is made to the duty of the clergy, readers and lay-workers to proclaim the Gospel and to explain the Christian Faith in appropriate ways. After this there is a return to a theology of worship in which activity the ministers obviously have a special part. Two points are made which few Christians will contest.

First, when ministers and people engage in worship, this both strengthens them for witness and service and is a forum in which Christ is made known. This probably means that in the listening to the reading of the Scriptures, especially of the Gospel, as well as to the Sermon and to the Eucharistic Prayer, there can be heard the Good News of the Father concerning his Incarnate Son and of the salvation available through and in him.

Secondly, worship is for all the people of God, ministers and others, and in this activity all are fellow pilgrims, journeying into "the heart of the love of God". The latter phrase is, however, not the best that could have been used to represent the goal and the end of the journey of pilgrims. As the hymn puts it, "We're marching upward to Zion / The beautiful City of God!"

Further, it is claimed that, as pilgrims, Christian people are at different stages of their journey to God. If by this is meant that baptized Christians are at different stages of maturity in the life of faith, hope and love then there can be no disagreement. However, in the rest of the paragraph the theme of pilgrimage appears to be closely connected to the presentation in certain services (especially Holy Baptism) of the Christian life in terms of stages, each of which is given liturgical symbolism. And the final stage seems to be "an opportunity of transformation". Outside the reference to Baptism, it probably is intended to convey the idea that liturgical worship is dynamic rather than static, unfolds in stages, and moves from gathering or assembling through transformation to sending out (*missio*). Obviously we have something here that seems to be very different in content and theme from the Services of Holy Baptism as well as the general ethos of worship in *The Book of Common Prayer*. Not only is the theme of "journeying" prominent in *Common Worship: Initiation Services* it is also the dominating image in the presentation of such services as visitation of the sick, marriage and burial of the dead in *Common Worship: Pastoral Services*.

7 *Diversity in Variety*

Common Worship *is marked by diversity, not only in its content and in those who will use it, but also in the manner of its publication. It is not a single book. This volume contains all that is needed for worship on Sundays and on Principal Feasts and Holy Days; the* Common Worship Initiation Services, Pastoral Services, Daily Office *book and seasonal material are being published separately. Moreover, these volumes are not published solely in book form.* Common Worship *is not a series of books, but a collection of services and other liturgical material published on the World Wide Web and through other electronic media as well as in print.*

All editions, printings and publishing of *The Book of Common Prayer* from 1549 to the 1970s were only in book form. Now it is available in electronic form at various websites and on CDs; but, it has always been *The Book of Common Prayer* for it is a Book devoted to Public and Common Prayer and the digital versions are versions of a book. Also *The Alternative Service Book 1980* was intended to be a book, given the title that belongs only to a book, and was a book throughout its twenty-year use.

What has been produced by the Church of England between 2000 and 2003 is deliberately not called *The Book of Common Worship*. Rather it is called *Common Worship* so that its actual content can be available in a variety of means of communication—book, booklet, card, CD, web site and so on. Yet everything within *Common Worship* is available in printed form of one kind or another (book, booklet and card), and from this base it is then available on CDs and at the Church of England Web Site. Apparently, however, the Preface, which is being quoted and examined here, is found only in the printed version of the main volume, the Sunday Service Book, as also is the Declaration of Assent cited above. Because of the digital and electronic revolution it is now relatively easy for parishes to produce their own services for all occasions by mechanical means and to tailor each service to their own requirements and devices. Thus what is common to all in this new era is the minimum and it relates to the use of common ingredients and common structures from a common store.

As noted above, the long list of authorized or commended Alternative Services (almost all of them *Common Worship* services) other than those of *The Book of Common Prayer* are listed on pp. 229–230 of the *Church of England Year Book 2003* as are the various volumes in which they are published. Together they constitute a veritable small library!

The principal Sunday-service volume of *Common Worship* is well printed on good opaque paper, and for the most part well-designed. At one critical point, however, the editors and designers demonstrate that they do not expect the book to be much read. The designer (appointed after "interviews conducted in Westminster Abbey's historic Jerusalem Chamber") "felt that the typeface for the Church of England's new worship book should be an English one,"[1] not a foreign creation, despite the ecumenical commitment of the same Church. Will the Church in Wales demand a Welsh-designed type-face? Does anyone feel culturally threatened by the use of Garamond or Bembo? There are, nevertheless, plenty of good English-designed fonts, including the one chosen, Gill Sans; but it is quite unsuitable for this job. A book with long passages of text to be read year in year out should not be set in a sans-serif face.[2] The *Companion* answers this objection by telling us that "The supposed greater legibility of serif over sans is not important because most of the prayers are lined out and there is not therefore much continuous text."[3] So lines of verse need not be as legible as prose? The greater legibility of serif is just a demonstrable fact. The *Companion* itself, for instance, could not have been set in sans, though it does use Gill Sans effectively for titling and running heads. Novels are never set in sans, and books of poetry, though "lined out", very rarely. A sans-serif Bible is unimaginable. Some sections of *Common Worship* have to be in bold, and "almost every serif bold is disappointing," the *Companion* tells us. This is not serious. What about Times New Roman Bold, an English face well used in current editions of the *Prayer Book*? Caslon

1 "The Design of Common Worship", *Companion to Common Worship*, vol. I, ed. Paul Bradshaw, 2001, pp. 255–6

2 The serifs, the little tags at the tops and bottoms of ascenders and descenders of letters, are found in all book-faces and aid legibility in smaller sizes. Sans-serif comes into its own with display sizes and posters.

3 *Companion*, p. 256. This was published before *Common Worship: Daily Prayer*, the 816-page volume which includes long passages of "lined-out" prose as well as ordinary prose and is intended for use "by an individual, a small group, a parish at prayer or a religious community" (p. viii). All 816 pages are set in Gill Sans.

Semibold (also an English design) is very good, though it is true that
Eric Gill's own beautiful serif typeface, Perpetua, does not go well into
bold. *Common Worship* would have been much better set in (the very
English) Stanley Morison's Times New Roman, or Bell, or Basker-
ville. The choice of Gill Sans and the remark about "lining out" show
how much continuous reading of the book its makers expect.

This "lining out" is another matter of concern. "Lining out"
originally meant the repetition of phrases by the congregation after
the priest, but is now used to refer to the practice of printing prose as
verse, with the aim of helping people to read it meaningfully. (Even
the tabloid papers still expect their vast audiences to be able to read
prose, but not the Church of England Liturgical Comission.)
Liturgical prayers in the Western tradition have always commonly
been in prose not verse, and the setting of them in this ultra-modern
way as if they were poetry not only confuses the reader's expectations
and invites verse reading, but also means that a tremendous amount
of paper is wasted. If the prayers were set as prose in an appropriate
typeface the whole of *Common Worship* would fit into not much more
than half the space that it now occupies, about 700 pages rather than
more than 1300, and would be much easier to read! The price could
also be substantially reduced.

The *Book of Common Prayer* was meant for daily worship and also
for private devotion, and was and is printed accordingly. Any
frequenter of second-hand bookshops will testify to the frequency of
well-worn copies. *Common Worship* is likely to remain in a much more
pristine condition.

8 *The Poetry of Praise and the Passion of Prayer*

Just as Common Worship *is more than a book, so worship is more than what
is said; it is also what is done and how it is done.* Common Worship *provides
texts, contemporary as well as traditional, which are resonant and memorable,
so that they will enter and remain in the Church of England's corporate
memory—especially if they are sung. It is when the framework of worship
is clear and familiar and the texts are known by heart that the poetry of
praise and the passion of prayer can transcend the printed word. Then
worship can take wing and become the living sacrifice of ourselves to the
God whose majesty is beyond compare and whose truth is from everlasting.*

Worship uses not only words (in rites) but also symbolic actions
(ceremonial). This paragraph makes this point and then leaves it
behind to focus only on the words, the texts. It claims for them that
they are "resonant and memorable" and as such will remain in the
"corporate memory" of the Church of England. This is surely to

exaggerate, for while one can immediately see that this claim can be, or is true, of the traditional texts from *The Book of Common Prayer,* one cannot likewise posit it to be true—at least at this early stage—of those texts which are of more recent vintage. Very little from *The Alternative Service Book 1980* has been judged to be resonant and memorable and so there is small likelihood of any improvement on this score with the texts of *Common Worship.* Time will tell.

The last two sentences of the paragraph, where we read of worship transcending the printed word and taking wing in ascent to the all-glorious and majestic God, are moving and contain profound practical truths. Yet the question arises as to whether these truths can be seen as applying to *Common Worship* which is all about variety, choice and sampling new possibilities, and where a fixed text to learn seems to be against the grain. In contrast, if one uses *The Book of Common Prayer* with its fixed texts then one can learn these by heart so that "the poetry of praise and the passion of prayer" can really begin (by God's grace) to transcend the printed page.

Summary

Before asking what further consideration of the themes of this Preface is necessary, it will be useful to recall the Preface to *The Alternative Service Book 1980* to see how it compares with the one written twenty years later.

The Preface of 1980 begins by explaining the status of the new Service Book. It is a supplement to *The Book of Common Prayer* (1662) of which it states: "It is a remarkable fact that for over three hundred years ... the Book of Common Prayer has remained the acknowledged norm for public worship in the Church of England." However, we are also informed that new conditions make it desirable that new understandings of worship should find expression in new forms and styles. Thus the provision of alternative services, created during a process of fifteen years of liturgical experiment, is (we are told) to be welcomed as an enrichment of the Church's life rather than a threat to its integrity. The services conform, it is claimed, to the doctrinal standard which is grounded in the Scriptures, expressed in the Creeds and expounded in the Anglican Formularies.

The 1980 Preface ends in this humble and promising way:

> But words, even agreed words, are only the beginning of worship. Those who use them do well to recognize their transience and imperfection; to treat them as a ladder, not a goal; to acknowledge their power in shaping faith and kindling devotion, without claiming that they are fully adequate to the task. Only the grace of God can make up what is lacking in the faltering words of

men. It is in reliance on such grace that this book is offered to the Church, in the hope that God's people may find in it a means in our day to worship him with honest minds and thankful hearts.

Comparing the two Prefaces, that of 1980 gives the impression of greater coherence of content and argument. Further, it makes humbler claims about what it is and can achieve. Yet, it only lasted twenty years.

Now we must return to the Preface of 2000 to ask what major themes and topics arise from its content which merit further detailed consideration. First of all, the title "Common Worship" which is similar to but different from "Common Prayer" calls for attention. We shall need to look at the use and meaning of both words, "Common" and "Worship". As certain themes of a theology of worship are proclaimed in the Preface, we shall bear these in mind as we look at the meaning of "worship". Especially we shall have to ask whether the Lord Jesus Christ and his relation to the Father in life, death, resurrection and exaltation is truly central.

In the second place, since "The Declaration of Assent" is referred to on two occasions, and by it ministers commit themselves to the official doctrines of the Church in public worship, the question arises as to whether the new services are in fact of the same doctrine as that contained in the authoritative Formularies, to which "The Declaration of Assent" points.

Then, thirdly, since a variety of claims is made about the quality of the language used in the Services, we shall need to examine whether the new "contemporary" language is as efficient and appropriate as the "traditional" language has been in creating the right medium for addressing and speaking of God, the Holy Trinity. Further, there is the related question as to whether a Prayer Book should mix the two styles of the language of prayer.

As much is made of Christians as pilgrims and of the relation of the journey to such services as Holy Communion (the Eucharist) and Holy Baptism, it will be necessary for us to look at both Eucharistic theology and also what is often these days called "the theology/liturgy of initiation". Also, as the journey takes all to an ending, we need to look at the Funeral service, and as the journey often goes *via* matrimony we need to look at the Marriage service.

Finally, by this Preface we are challenged to consider whether a Church with a long tradition of Common Prayer has gone to great lengths, and using a variety of means of communication, to make it nearly impossible for there to be Common Prayer in the Church of England in the future. That is, is "Common Worship" merely a Name provided to make us feel good about the demise and disappearance of Common Prayer?

CHAPTER TWO

An Examination of "Common"

We have noted that in 2000 the Church of England replaced her *Alternative Service Book 1980* with *Common Worship: Services and Prayers for the Church of England*. Further we have also noted that this title refers not to one book but to several books and booklets; it is not found on one CD but on two or three; it is not a fixed or final text but an evolutionary one, created for possible change when needs arise as the years go by. The official reason given in the introductory pamphlet for the new publication was that "our world is constantly changing and our understanding of God is always developing. God may not change, but in every generation we find new ways of expressing ourselves to one another and to God."[1]

Yet despite changing human ideas of God's identity, and maybe change in God as God in relation to the cosmos (if it be that process theology is in mind here), the Church of England also confirmed in 2000 that the "ancient" English Prayer Book, *The Book of Common Prayer* (1662), remained in place as the first Prayer Book and primary Formulary of the Church.[2] No Synod of the Church has any authority to change or remove it, and, conversely, no parish is required to use it, although many do so, as also do virtually all Cathedrals.

Thus at the beginning of the third millennium the Church of England offers to her members choice of which book to use, and in the new book, which service amongst several to choose. The publicity that surrounded the launch of *Common Worship* appeared to suggest that public worship using a rite from either this book or *The Book of Common Prayer* fits under the umbrella of "Common Public Worship" or belongs to the genre of "Common Prayer". In fact, "common prayer" is defined as "shared forms of worship".

The full title of the new rites probably provides the basic definition of what is officially understood today as "common worship". The colon separating "Common Worship" from "Services

1 *Common Worship: Planning for Change*, The Liturgical Publishing Group, 2000, Part I
2 *Ibid.*

23

and Prayers for the Church of England" is perhaps to be seen as a sign of equality and equivalency. Therefore, whatever are the officially approved services and prayers, whenever and however they appear, these are what we are to take as common worship and even common prayer. One could perhaps say in a moment of cynicism that "Common" is now being used as a conjuring word, rather than as a specific word with a specific meaning. To render liturgical documents valid, they must have the word "common" pronounced over them, much like a magician's "abracadabra," without any sense of the word's original meaning.

What is meant by "Common"?

Since we are referring to the worship of Almighty God, we can dismiss quickly the popular meaning of "common" as that which is ordinary or undistinguished or even of inferior quality. The texts of the services and rites are intended to be of high not low quality. The basic meaning of "common" as used in religious English appears to be "that in which the people unite". Thus Common Worship or Common Prayer is public worship/prayer in which people unite in the public place for worship using an approved form of service.

Before and at the publishing of *The Book of the Common Prayer and Administration of the Sacraments and other rites and ceremonies of the Church: after the use of the Church of England* (1549) "common prayer" referred to the Daily Offices said by the clergy and some laity in the chancel of the church. Since this was not the private office of the clergy but the public gathering of the people of the parish, it was "common prayer", offered to God in Latin until 1549 and in English thereafter. The long title of the English Prayer Book was necessary, for it replaced the multiple service books (Breviary, Missal, Manual etc.) of the late medieval period, books which provided what is known as "the Sarum Use".

We may note that the title, *The Book of the Common Prayer ... after the use of the Church of England,* presupposes that there is a form of prayer "common" (both because necessary and the actual historical case under the Providence of God) to the whole Christian Church. What Archbishop Cranmer offered in English was the presentation of that "common" (taken as "universal") prayer of the Christian Church after the use of a particular national church, the Church of England.

In 1552, the second definite article was removed so that the title began, *The Book of Common Prayer* and from this time forwards the expression "Common Prayer" gradually came to mean all the public services in which the people united, including the public celebration of the sacraments. Further, the expression "Common Prayer" also came to mean the actual book that contained the services. Thus the expression "Common Prayer" in everyday conversation came to mean both a specific text containing services or rites and the assembling and uniting of the clergy and people to use these services to pray and worship publicly.

In the official *Book of Homilies* (1562) of the Church of England, there are several sermons which deal with prayer. One of these is entitled, "An Homily wherein is declared that Common Prayer and Sacraments ought to be administered in a tongue that is understanded of the hearers". After explaining two kinds of prayer, the silent prayer of the heart and the vocal, private prayer, we are told:

> The third sort of Prayer is Public or Common. Of this Prayer speaketh our Saviour Christ when he saith, *If two of you shall agree upon earth upon any thing, whatsoever ye shall ask, my Father which is in heaven shall do it for you; for, wheresoever two or three be gathered together in my name, there am I in the midst of them.* ... By the histories of the Bible it appeareth that Public and Common Prayer is most available before God; and therefore it is much to be lamented that it is no better esteemed among us, which profess to be but one body in Christ. ... Let us join ourselves together in the place of Common Prayer, and with one voice and one heart beg of our heavenly Father all those things which he knoweth to be necessary for us. I forbid you not private prayer, but I exhort you to esteem Common Prayer as it is worthy.[1]

Here Common Prayer is that praise and supplication offered to God the Father with one heart and voice by the one body of Christ in the place appointed for worship.

In the Fifth Book of *The Laws of Ecclesiastical Polity*, written towards the end of the Elizabethan era, Richard Hooker, the distinguished apologist for the Church of England against Puritanism, defended and commended the official English version of "Common Prayer" as found in *The Book of Common Prayer* (edition of 1559) against the criticisms of the Puritans. For him, as for the homilist, "Common Prayer" is the worship of Almighty God with one heart and voice by the one body in the one place, using a language that all understand as that is found in the English *Prayer Book*. The preaching services of the Puritans and Presbyterians are not "common prayer" even though Christian people genuinely hear the Word of God and give assent to prayer offered to heaven by the preacher.

In reference to the consecrated church building and its association with common prayer, Hooker wrote:

---

1 *Certain Sermons or Homilies*, repr. 1899, pp. 375–6

And concerning the place of assembly, although it serve for other uses as well as this ... the principal cause thereof must needs be in regard of Common Prayer ... that there we stand, we pray, we sound forth hymns unto God, having his angels intermingled as our associates ... . But of all helps for due performance of this service the greatest is that very set and standing order itself, which framed with common advice, hath both for matter and form prescribed whatever is herein publicly done. No doubt from God it hath proceeded, and by us it must be acknowledged a work of his singular care and providence, that the Church hath evermore held a prescript form of common prayer, although not in all things everywhere the same, yet for the most part retaining still the same analogy.[1]

For Hooker "that very set and standing order itself" is Common Prayer, *The Book of Common Prayer* (1559) authorized by Queen Elizabeth I.

One of the basic characteristics of the traditional English Common Prayer has been that one only rite is provided for each of the public services and there is no provision for extempore prayer by the minister. While the readings from the Holy Scripture change daily, the actual service itself is virtually identical daily and weekly. There is no optional rite for Holy Communion or Baptism or the Daily Services of Morning and Evening Prayer. Thus Common Prayer also developed the meaning of the use of a common text not only in the one parish church but in all the churches of the one nation. And this of course was what the various Acts of Uniformity meant and required.

It is important to recognize the ordinary English sense of the identity of Common Prayer with the book of the same name.

Common Prayer belongs to the nation; it was created for us out of, and taking theological exception to, various departmental service-books and other documents; it was recovered for us, in defiance of the Presbyterian Directory, in 1662; it was retained for us, in defiance of William III's desired "comprehension" (a sort of "home-centres" ecumenical venture ...) [in 1689]; it comfortably resisted Unitarian depredations in the 18th century; it was the linch-pin of the Tractarian movement; it was only cautiously modified in 1928, in an attempt to keep the Anglo-Catholics away from the lure of the English Missal. The book belongs to us all, even if only a tiny proportion of the tiny proportion that attends church today actually prays it ... .[2]

Common Prayer ordinarily means the public worship of the

1 *Of the Laws of Ecclesiastical Polity*, Book V, Chapter 25, paras. 2, 4
2 A. C. Capey, "Common Prayer and the Pirates" in *The Real Common Worship*, ed. Peter Mullen, Denton, 2000, pp. 68–9

assembled Christian congregations within churches and cathedrals using services taken from *The Book of Common Prayer*. Common Prayer does not refer to any kind of public prayer but only to that which is according to the form provided by this prayer book. This important principle has been enforced and underlined by the practice, which began in 1552, of printing the Act for the Uniformity of Common Prayer inside *The Book of Common Prayer*. The 1662 Act may be read in many editions of the *Prayer Book*, and explanations of it are offered in the twenty or more annotated editions that appeared in the nineteenth and early part of the twentieth century.[1]

Our reasons for emphasizing the identity of Common Prayer and *The Book of Common Prayer* will become clearer later in this chapter.

A Godly Way of Life

It is important to grasp that the contents of *The Book of the Common Prayer* were more than a translation, adaptation, and renewal of the medieval services of prayer and worship. They reached behind the Middle Ages and witnessed to the recovery of a godly ordering of the whole of life on earth from birth to death, 365 days a year, within the discipline and rhythms of the Church Year with its weekly Lord's Day and its Feasts and Fasts. The Common Prayer of the universal Church, as given structure and form in the offices and services of *The Book of the Common Prayer*, became the Anglican Way of relating to God, in a national Church with her dioceses, colleges, schools, families, and baptized members. The Common Prayer became the model of an entire life lived in communion with God, the Father, through his Son our Lord and Saviour Jesus Christ, by the indwelling of the Holy Ghost.

In Mattins and Evensong the medieval daily offices (Mattins, Lauds, Prime, Terce, Sext, None, Vespers, and Compline) were compressed into two. What had previously been seen as primarily the business of clergy, monks, and nuns was now available in English and recommended for all. At their local church or in their homes, all people could now be joined by the Holy Ghost to the communion of saints, together with the angels and archangels, in offering daily worship to God on behalf of the whole created order. United to Jesus Christ the Head of the Body, they could pray the Psalter morning and evening as the intelligent members of the Body of Christ. And on Wednesdays and Fridays, as well as on Sundays, they could intercede for one another by joining in the Litany.

1 E. g., see *The Prayer Book Interleaved* with notes by W. M. Campion & W. J. Beaumont, 1866 and later editions.

On Sundays and Feasts, as well as on other days of solemn obligation, all could hear the liturgy in English, including a sermon or homily. Parish priests not competent to prepare a sermon themselves were required to read a homily from the *Certain Sermons or Homilies* (1547 & 1562). If duly prepared, the people could receive the Holy Communion in both kinds, just as their priest did.

At each of the Daily Offices were readings from both the Old and the New Testaments. At the Holy Communion there were the Epistle and Gospel, together with a Psalm for each Sunday and Feast. Great emphasis was therefore placed upon the Christian duty of hearing and reading the Holy Scripture, followed by meditating upon the same, to be completed by obeying it as the Word of God in daily living.

Thus the Common Prayer is a biblical, traditional, and godly way for the congregation, Christian family, and individual baptized believer to relate to God the Holy Trinity as the disciples of the Lord Jesus Christ, in the fellowship of the one, holy, catholic, and apostolic Church within God's world, 365 days a year and every year of the present age.

The basis of the Common Prayer is the daily offering of praise through the daily offices wherein the Psalms (the prayers of Jesus Christ) are central, as is the meditative reading of all the Holy Scriptures. Linked to this is the petitionary and intercessory prayer of the Litany, along with the celebration of the symbolic meal of the new covenant in the Eucharist on each Lord's Day and on the other holy days. In the Holy Communion the Church is fed and strengthened by heavenly manna as she communes with her Bridegroom.

Then Common Prayer makes provision for thanking God for the entry of a child into the world (the churching of women); for the entry of that child into the church of God (holy baptism and confirmation); and for that child's grown-up entry into the holy state of matrimony. Add to this the provisions for the visitation of the sick and the burial of the dead, and here is a total way of life for the faithful people of God on this earth.

This Common Prayer is common because it is the norm for *all* people wherever they are and whatever their status in life. There can be a minimal participation or a maximal participation by persons, families and congregations. The basic structure and uniformity are necessary in order to train us in good habits and right discipline; they are also necessary to help us know what is freedom and how it is to be exercised within our duty to God and our neighbour.

So the Common Prayer is a godly order for the people of the Anglican Way, and it is expressed and set forth in a series of editions of *The Book of Common Prayer* in English (1549 through to [Canada] 1962), as well as in many editions in many languages around the world. In most of these editions the basis is the 1662 *Book of Common Prayer*, to which local prayers and forms are added by the various national churches.

The Book of Common Prayer has been always a Formulary of the Anglican Way since it expresses the doctrinal commitment of the Church of England and of the Anglican Communion of Churches to the worship and service of the Father almighty, through his only begotten Son, and with the Holy Ghost. *Lex orandi, lex credendi* (the law of praying is the law of believing, and the law of believing is the law of praying) is a principle that is fundamental to the Anglican Way.

Modifications of *The Book of Common Prayer* through its several editions in English and in many other languages (beginning with Latin in the early days of Elizabeth I, when that was the common tongue of the universities and schools) are to be expected as the Common Prayer is adapted to changing cultures and societies and times. These local modifications (e. g., praying for a President and not a Monarch and incorporating local, national holidays) do not take away from the traditional commitment of the Anglican churches to a single godly order for all. The Church welcomes everyone into this order, whether an archbishop or a new member; a king, a queen, a president, or a commoner; a man or a woman; a teenager or a grandparent.

The expansion of the meaning of "Common"

In the light of the long history and use of the Common Prayer, it is not surprising that in England in the 1970s when new types and shapes of services using "contemporary" language were collected together into a new prayer book, the decision was taken to call the collection *The Alternative Service Book*. In Canada much the same type of book was called *The Book of Alternative Services* (1985). These books contained multiple options so that the idea of "a common text" and "common rite" had disappeared from them. From now on, it seemed that the only way that "common" could be used of public worship was in the sense of an act of worship in which people freely unite together.

But before 1980 a new approach to "common" had already been pioneered and had triumphed in the Episcopal Church of the USA. Here in 1979 had appeared the revision of the 1928 American *Prayer Book*, and, although this 1979 book was very much like the English *Alternative Service Book*, and contained variety not uniformity, it was nevertheless given the title, *The Book of Common Prayer*. From the richest and possibly most influential province of the Anglican Communion apart from England, a powerful message was being sent to all the Anglican Family. It was this: "Common" has changed its meaning. At this early stage American and British English were not in step with each other but the Brits were soon to catch up!

Liturgists and bishops did not apparently want to let the use of the word "common" go from their liturgical revisions and innovations. So emphasis began to be placed upon "a common structure" meaning the "Shape of the Liturgy" (the title of an influential book by Gregory Dix first published in 1945) into which agreed structure differing forms of words could be inserted, so that there could be multiple choice of content, e. g., of the prayer of consecration in the Eucharist. Further, emphasis was also placed upon "common texts" referring to the use of such basic items as the Lord's Prayer, the Sanctus, the Sursum Corda, the Gloria and so on which should be a part of all Eucharistic Liturgy. Thus it became acceptable in the 1980s to refer to the increasing provision of varied rites and services as belonging to "common worship" and even to "common prayer". What was happening was that "common" was being loosed from its connection with uniformity, and thus with the fixed texts of *The Book of Common Prayer,* in order to function as a kind of catch-all for new liturgies that had the approved right shape and the appropriate basic content of common texts within that shape.

So efforts began to be made to make "common" mean "that which has been issued by common authority in a specific place". This alteration of meaning makes thinking people, even among enthusiasts for revision, nervous. The vague substitute of "a common shape" is a Band-Aid for this nervousness—it's not a cure, but it does cover it up a bit. The problem is, what does "a common shape" mean? One might think that "form" and "shape" are synonyms, but how can they be, if they mean different things?

And they do mean different things, since we are expected to believe that "a common shape" exists apart from a common form defined by its common content, common vocabulary, common syntax, common order, and common intention to say the same things. What's left may be "a shape common to human worship", but it isn't necessarily a form of worship common to Christianity. One could, no doubt, take the minimal shape of "An Order for Celebrating the Holy Eucharist" and use it to construct a service for the worship of Krishna or Baal. A "shape" of worship may look similar to Christian worship without being Christian worship.

No doubt, the influence of Gregory Dix, with his antipathy towards the *Book of Common Prayer,* has been important here. He used the idea of a "shape" as a way to justify the abandonment of the English

Common Prayer tradition, and others have since applied it in even more extreme ways. Dix's original training was as a lawyer, and one could argue that his idea of "shape" has more in common with a lawyer's pleading, in which he attempts to find a construction of the evidence or a conceptual basis to win his case, than with impartial scholarship.[1]

In England we can trace the attempt by the Liturgical Commission and others to follow the initial American lead and to remove "Common Prayer" as the sole property of *The Book of Common Prayer*. Let us begin in 1989 with the publication *Patterns of Worship*. Under the heading of "Common Prayer?" we are told that

> "Common Prayer" does not in fact exist, in the sense of being able to walk into any church in the land and find exactly the same words to follow. Nor should we pretend that it would be either right or good to return to a position—well over a century ago—when that might have been the case. Rather, "common prayer" exists in the Church of England in the sense of recognizing, as one does when visiting members of the same family, some common features, some shared experiences, languages and patterns of tradition.[2]

Then we are provided with a list of "the marks which should be safeguarded" by those who wish to stand in any recognizable continuity with historical Anglican tradition. These are

   1 A recognizable structure for worship;

   2 An emphasis on reading the word and on using psalms;

   3 Liturgical words used by the congregation, some of which, like the creed, would be known by heart;

   4 The use of a collect, the Lord's Prayer, and some responsive form in prayer;

   5 A recognition of the centrality of the Eucharist, and

   6 A concern for form, dignity and economy of words.

(Moving on to *Common Worship* we note that the first Service in the whole collection is "A Service of the Word [with a Celebration of Holy Communion]" which is provided only as an outline or shape rather than as a full liturgy.)

The Worship of the Church[3] makes a conscious attempt to draw together the new tradition of variety as in *The Alternative Service Book 1980* and the old tradition of uniformity as in *The Book of Common Prayer* (1662). There is a plea for "a unitive doctrinal

---

   1 See further Louis Bouyer, *Liturgical Piety* [French, 1954; English, 1955], pp. 275–6 for early, if polite, doubt about Dix's hypothetical constructions.

   2 *Patterns of Worship*, p. 5. Note the two floating participial clauses from authors charged with composing the liturgy of the Church of England.

   3 GS Misc. 364, 1991

sensitivity" and a "sense of Common Prayer" which would require the use of the *Prayer Book* alongside the new liturgies. "Common Prayer" is seen as including both new and old, and this Report clearly distinguishes "Common Prayer" from *The Book of Common Prayer* in order to make the new services belong to it.

In 1993 there was published *The Renewal of Common Prayer: Unity and Diversity in Church of England Worship,* which is a collection of essays by the members of the 1991–6 Commission and edited by Michael Perham. Here an attempt is made to define for the century soon to dawn what "common prayer" might mean. A "proper balance" between commonality of text on the one hand, and variety, diversity and spontaneity on the other is discussed. There is talk of a common core, a common shape, a common structure, and common contents but in it all a rejection of the traditional and classic understanding and meaning of "Common Prayer" as that which is inside the covers of the *Prayer Book.* Nevertheless the *Prayer Book* itself continued to be treated with respect.

This respect is reflected in the publication of *Model and Inspiration* (1993), which contains the major contributions to a symposium held on 5 November 1992 in London. Two of these were made by two prominent members of the Prayer Book Society, Professor David Martin, the sociologist, and Baroness James of Holland Park, the novelist. Apparently it was at this conference that the idea that the replacement to *The Alternative Service Book 1980* should include both a variety of new liturgies and, importantly, the major texts from the *Prayer Book,* gained wide acceptance.

A further, major influence on the changing or expanding of the meaning of "Common Prayer" came from 1992 onwards with the availability of *Celebrating Common Prayer.* Two members of the Commission, Bishop David Stancliffe and Brother Tristam SSF, had worked with members of religious communities, especially the Society of St Francis, to produce this daily office book wherein is great variety of usage for different days and seasons. At the Lambeth Conference of Bishops held at the University of Canterbury in 1998, the Archbishop of Canterbury gave to all the 900 or so bishops a copy of this book for which he (George Carey) had written a Foreword. In this he claimed that Morning and Evening Prayer from *The Book of Common Prayer* were not widely used and Anglicans therefore needed a pattern of daily prayer, which the Franciscan provision would adequately satisfy. Thus this book could provide them with real or celebratory "common prayer" which the *Book* of that name could not do.

Thus it is not at all surprising to find that when we get to the publicity material for *Common Worship* (2000) we are told that this collection of services and resources "emphasizes the important part that worship plays in expressing our unity. It is something that we have in 'common'." Here "common" seems to mean "worship in the Church of England based upon one or another of the services, or using the provided resources, of the collection known as *Common Worship*".[1] Thus "common" now has a Congregationalist meaning, referring to the particular liturgy that is devised locally for use locally in a parish—and the very first outline of a service in the main volume of Common Worship entitled "A Service of the Word" is intended for this Congregationalist purpose.

From the Liturgical Commission in 2002 came *New Patterns for Worship*, a book containing material from *Common Worship* together with other texts and advice on the construction of services. This publication updated the earlier *Patterns for Worship* of 1989. Under the heading, "Common Prayer in the Church of England" three aspects of "the Anglican understanding of common prayer are stated":

> 1 The valuing of patterns of worship which are recognized as the common possession of the people of God. This does not mean that nothing can change nor that every popular practice must prevail. It does not rule out any local variation. It does mean that worship must not simply be governed by the whim of the minister or the congregation. Corporate patterns of worship must exist and be developed which are recognized by worshippers as their corporate worship. It is therefore appropriate that these are approved and regulated by the Church.
>
> 2 The patterns and forms of worship must not be determined purely at the level of the local congregation but must bear witness to participation in the wider common life of the Church. For this reason it is right that common forms such as creeds, collects, confessions and eucharistic prayers should be followed, as well as common approaches to the shape and content of Christian worship.
>
> 3 Patterns of common prayer play an important part in maintaining the unity of the Church in its confession of the Christian faith.[2]

This usefully summarizes the doctrine of the Liturgical Commission concerning common prayer and clearly reveals the substantial change of meaning that has occurred in a period of twenty-five years or so. Interestingly, the new meaning of "common prayer" is made more explicit in the section giving guidance for discussion groups.[3] They are to work under two headings, "Structures and Texts" and the marks which should be safeguarded to preserve Anglican common

---

1 *Common Worship: Planning for Change*, Part I
2 *New Patterns for Worship*, p.51   3 p. 53

prayer are still said to be much as *Patterns for Worship* reported them fourteen years earlier[1]—a recognizable structure for worship; an emphasis on reading the word and on using the psalms; liturgical words repeated by the congregation, some of which like the creed, would be known by heart; using a collect, the Lord's Prayer, and some responsive forms in prayer; a recognition of the centrality of the Eucharist; a concern for form, dignity and economy of words.

We noted above that in 1979 the Episcopal Church of the USA chose to call its book of alternative services, containing both traditional and contemporary language rites, *The Book of Common Prayer, according to the use of the Episcopal Church*, and the Church in the West Indies did the same thing in 1995, calling its modern language edition of alternative services, *The Book of Common Prayer, according to the use of the Church of the West Indies*; but the General Synod of the Church of England, knowing that *The Book of Common Prayer* (1662) refers to a specific text that cannot be removed as a Formulary, came as near as it could, within the law, to using the old title for its new collection. It may be noted that *Common Worship* is as near to *Common Prayer* as you can get! However, it is not *The Book of Common Worship* but *Common Worship*, for it is available in a variety of forms, printed and digital, and is open-ended.

A Wrong Path

The advent of new prayer books and the changing use of the word "common" have affected worldwide Anglicanism in the international Anglican Communion of Churches. Wherever one went in the world up to the 1970s, one could find an Anglican church and recognize, even if the language was not English and whatever the church-manship, the use of *The Book of Common Prayer*. One may claim that the glue that united the Anglican Communion was the use of an edition of the *Prayer Book*, even though that book was used in over 150 languages and dialects, apart from English. Now, in contrast to the period up to 1970, we find that the Anglican Communion is no longer seen as united through the Common Formulary of the *Prayer Book* and a commonly recognized Ministry. World travellers in the new millennium do not know what to expect at an Anglican church, not only in different countries but even in one's own country! There has been a most noticeable move away from both the liturgy and the doctrine of the *Prayer Book*.

Much emphasis is laid today upon the Instruments of Unity—the See of Canterbury, the Lambeth Conference every ten years, the annual Primates' Meeting and the regular meeting of the Anglican

1 See above, p. 31.

Consultative Council. One reason for this great emphasis upon instruments is that of compensating, at least in part, for the loss of unity in how Anglicans worship together, caused by the relegation of the historic *Prayer Book* to one option amongst many. Further, the commonly recognized Ministry is no longer emphasised because not all Provinces recognize women bishops (or even women presbyters) and because the original Common Text for Ordinations (= the Ordinal in *The Book of Common Prayer*) is rarely used. Yet, as we have already noted with respect to England, the Anglican Communion also seems to want to hang on to the word "Common" and look for anything that has the potential for uniting as coming within the definition of "common".

But let us consider the possibility that it would have been far better, and basically more honest, if the word "common" (as a prominent and dominant adjective) had been retained for use solely and only with the authentic *Book of Common Prayer* and the public worship using the rites from this book. Certainly, not to have used this adjective of the expanding new rites and services, or of certain fixed parts of them, would have helped to make clear the major differences between the shape, language and content of the services within *The Book of Common Prayer* and the shape, language and content of the services found in the vast collection of prayer books published since the 1970s. After all, the modern rites are virtually all in so-called "contemporary language" in contrast to "traditional language", and as we shall see, their structure, or shape, is different, as is also the doctrinal emphasis therein, from that of the classical *Prayer Book*.

The decision by liturgists, bishops and synods to retain the word "common" (as in *Common Worship* and *Celebrating Common Prayer*) for that which in practical terms are not single common texts and services but the very opposite—multiple choice texts and services adapted to local needs—means that "common" in the sense long used in the idiom of religious English is in danger of being lost. Some may think that this is a good thing, or a normal thing in that language develops. Others may think that since *The Book of Common Prayer* is still the official Prayer Book of the Church of England there was a duty laid upon bishops especially to retain the word "common" for use with this classic Book and to choose other appropriate words for descriptions of the new services.

In 1980 when *The Alternative Service Book* was published in England, no claims were made in England that here was common prayer or common worship. Yet, as we noted above, at about the same time, across the Atlantic ocean, the Episcopal Church of the USA published its collection of services, in traditional and contemporary language, and for it used the historic title, *The Book of Common Prayer*. In so doing the same Church declared that the authentic Anglican form of common prayer, found in its own *Book of Common Prayer* (1928) was no longer to be used. Thus we have from 1979 the move, which later caught on in the rest of the Anglican Churches of the West/North, to change or enlarge the meaning of "common" so that its meaning as understood for long centuries has been pushed into the background. Now it seems anything can be common prayer or common worship if it is a service that loosely follows guidelines produced by any diocese or province in the Anglican Communion of Churches.

But why should the retention for public use of the word "common" in reference to liturgy be so important to the leadership of the modern Anglican churches? Since 1979 they have gone to great lengths to retain it, even when they must have known they were not being faithful to the Anglican tradition of usage. It would seem that they have a deep desire to believe and to claim that what they are producing, commending and authorizing is somehow, or ought to be in reality, a genuine continuation of the English public prayer and worship that has gone before. That is, they are claiming that their modern forms of worship are the true successors of what Archbishop Cranmer had in mind when he spearheaded the revolution to render the Latin rites in multiple books into English rites in one book. What Cranmer and his co-operators did in 1548–52 for their time and generation, modern liturgists believe or at least claim that they are doing for theirs. They like him claim that they are ministering to the needs of the time. Thus they can attempt to justify their use of the adjective that was chosen in 1549 to appear in the first edition of the first ever authorized Prayer Book in English. It may be the case, however, that modern liturgists and bishops instinctively felt that their relation to and ties with the history of English Liturgy were at best so tenuous that it was desireable to retain this word for their innovations, to divert public attention from the weakness of this link. In this connection they have been not altogether unreasonably called "pirates" by some people.[1]

In that there are such great differences between *The Book of Common Prayer* and the books of Alternative Services in "contemporary" English, it would have been far better had the borrowing of this important word not occurred. The presence of the word "common" in the title of very different collections of liturgy—from the American 1979 *Prayer Book* to *Common Worship*—is one of those factors that bring confusion and uncertainty into the modern Church, to the detriment of spiritual edification and general understanding.

1 E. g. A. C. Capey, *op. cit.*

In fact, the decision by the General Synod of the Church of England to include within its *Common Worship* certain services from *The Book of Common Prayer* (which remains permanently authorized as the primary Prayer Book of the Church in its own independent right by the Act of Uniformity) seems at first sight a strange decision. And on second sight a bad and wrong decision, even an outrageous one.

One can ask, If these services are so easily available why print them (howbeit in edited form) all over again, and add to the size of the already over-size *Common Worship*? The easy answer is that by placing versions of the most used services of the *Prayer Book* in *Common Worship* there became available in one source at one place all the major services currently authorized for use in the Church. One consequence could be (as perhaps some liturgists and bishops hope) that the *Prayer Book* itself will fall into disuse and die a natural death—despite its place as a Formulary of the Church. Another answer could be the desire to present a comprehensive assortment of choice of services. After all, as long as there is in public view and use a prayer book which has the title, *The Book of Common Prayer*, a basic question mark is likely to be placed after the title, *Common Worship*, at least by some people. Better to get parishes to put into dark cupboards their old copies of the *Prayer Book*, or better still, recycle their pages, as with the recently departed *Alternative Service Book*. From another perspective, the presence of the ancient texts along with the modern texts in one book or on one CD reinforces the modern attempt to change the meaning of the expression "Common Prayer".

But from the standpoint of the *Prayer Book* itself, as has been explained above, its content is a unified whole and belongs together. It contains a godly order for family, parish, and nation, an order that covers and provides for the whole of life and the whole of the Christian Year. To divide the contents of the *Prayer Book* and place some in another book is to cut apart this godly order. Those who use *The Book of Common Prayer* faithfully with understanding and piety believe that they are by God's grace participating in this godly order for life here on earth in preparation for life above in the age to come. They believe that by the mercy and providence of God they are in the genuine English tradition of Common Prayer.

CHAPTER THREE

An Examination of "Worship"

True Christian worship is the consecration and use of all our faculties to the glory of the Holy Trinity and in his service. It is the joyous abasement of the people of God before the Divine Mystery, who is the Triune God. While it can be claimed that worship like prayer is to be unceasing, the Church has always had fixed times on the Lord's Day and during the week for what it has presented as Common Prayer or Public Worship.

The adoration, praise, thanksgiving, confession, intercession, petition, consecration and dedication offered by the Church as a united Body and her members individually to God the Father through and in the name of the Lord Jesus Christ and with the Holy Ghost are what we call "the worship of God". This holy activity involves Word and Sacrament, Ritual and Ceremonial.

A Liturgical Revolution

The story of the Liturgical Movement in the Roman Catholic Church and then in the Protestant Churches, including the Anglican Communion of Churches, during the twentieth century, has often been told. For the purpose of understanding changing definitions of and approaches to Christian worship in the Church of England in the twentieth century, we cannot avoid taking note of what happened from the late 1960s onwards including such things as the publication of *The Alternative Service Book 1980* and a variety of official worship booklets afterwards, the entry of the pentecostalist or charismatic movement into the mainline churches, the major changes in styles of worship in the Roman Catholic Church, the influence of feminism on the way in which the churches make use of women and also speak of and address Deity, and the emergence of new forms of theology producing novel types of theism (such as process theology and panentheism) which have affected the way many people think of the relation of God to the world and to people.

In general, what this has meant is that clergy and congregations have become more vitally concerned with the God who is immanent and less conscious of the God who is transcendent. That is, the God who is immediate and friendly is more sought and recognized than the God who is holy and majestic. Thus acts of worship have become more informal and participatory and less clergy-dominated and led. There is also a much greater variety between parishes as each chooses its own text, rite and style. Further, the ways participants dress and their manner of addressing God have moved from the formal to the informal. The language used on the streets and in the media is now the language of worship, in contrast to the traditional sacred language of worship and prayer. That is, God is now the "You-God" not the "Thou-God" in accordance with the belief that the familiar language makes God more real.

Major themes that have influenced, and to some degree, have been incorporated into public worship and religious language include an emphasis upon relevance, accessibility, simplicity; the need for variety; a keen interest in community (cf. the oft-used "community of faith"); celebration as being a communal experience and thus with more standing and less kneeling; adaptation of early church practices (e. g. the kiss of peace) to encourage mutuality and togetherness; the self-esteem movement and psychotherapy (the importance of feeling good about oneself and about worship); a making of women visible (in ministry and in the use of words for God); inclusivity of all types of persons so that there are no outcasts; freedom and liberation; peace and justice movements;[1] ecumenical agreements and common texts; concern for the environment and creation; use of modern music with the move from organ to more popular instruments; creating "a personal relationship with God", and so on.

In the liturgical and synodical preparation for the replacement of *The Alternative Service Book* by what came to be called *Common Worship* what were seen as the gains since the 1960s were taken for granted and allowed to flow into the context, structure and content of the new collection of rites, services, creeds and prayers for the Church of England. That is, the approach to worship in *Common Worship* cannot be understood and appreciated unless the liturgical, doctrinal and ethical achievements of the second half of the twentieth century are taken into account. So it is not surprising that *A Companion to Common Worship,* Volume 1 (2001) has been published and Volume 2 is promised.

To express the matter in a more technical way one can say that after the secular reductionism of the 1960s, liturgical scholars have tended since the 1970s to maintain a stress on the humanity of

1 See the "baptismal covenant", below, Chapter Six.

worship but have tried to balance this through a regaining of the
sense of rites and signs as vehicles of transcendence from and
towards God. To this end they have sought and continue to seek
useful tools in phenomenology, cultural anthropology, and semiotics
while at the same time not forgetting or recognizing the divine
component in the system, structure or pattern of "communication"
which is Christian liturgy.

In the Foreword to Volume 1 of the *Companion to Common Worship*
the Bishop of Salisbury, who is the "chair" of the Liturgical
Commission, states:

> The text of *Common Worship* with its rubrics provides a template
> for the Church's worship. But this template needs an interpret-
> ative guidebook. All those who are responsible for designing and
> leading any part of the Church's worship need to understand the
> theological, historical and liturgical background to the texts that
> have been painstakingly crafted and carefully scrutinized on the
> way to formal authorization.

Here the Bishop tells us that the contents of *Common Worship* are not
sufficiently clear in and of themselves to stand on their own but need
an interpretative guidebook. Thus even the local parish reader or
"praise leader" must study (this book) before they exercise their local
ministries. And since not all of us may be familiar with a template or
templet, it is an instrument used as a gauge or guide in bringing any
piece of work to the desired shape. Thus *Common Worship* is the
means of bringing the thoughts and deeds of the people of God to
the proper shape of the worship of God. Yet to use this template
aright we need the instructional manual, as it were, and the amount
of books we need grows. One significant recent manual is *New
Patterns For Worship*, an expanded and revised edition of *Patterns of
Worship* of 1989. This "how to do it" book is filled with instruction on
every conceivable aspect of producing from scratch a "family
service" or an "all-age service" or a thematic Eucharist or whatever.

Worship and Common Worship

It is much more difficult to ascertain and understand the nature and
content of worship in the varied collection of *Common Worship* than
in *The Book of Common Prayer*. This is because the former has a much
vaster range of services, prayers, creeds and bits and pieces to survey;
and within the services what is required and what is not required has
also to be taken in account. Then this collection comes from a variety
of sources, has known a variety of editorial hands, is relatively new
and is still growing.

In the Preface we noticed that several claims are made concerning the theology of worship. Perhaps the most important of these is this: "Central to our worship is the proclamation of the one, perfect, self-offering of the Son to the Father. The Gospel of Jesus Christ is at the heart of Christian worship." It is not clear whether "the Gospel of Jesus Christ" is meant to be the same as "the proclamation of the one, perfect self-offering ... " or whether they are related but distinct things.

Certainly the good news from God the Father concerning his Incarnate Son, the Lord Jesus Christ, who lived, died, rose again and ascended into heaven for us and for our salvation is presupposed and declared in the services.

Certainly also the self-offering of the Incarnate Son to the Father through his consecration to Messianic ministry, his obedience to the Father's will even unto the sentence of crucifixion, and his suffering and death for sinners are also presented in the services.

Having said this, one must also proceed to note that nowhere in the services of *Common Worship* that do not come from, or are not based directly upon, *The Book of Common Prayer*, is the active and passive suffering of Christ as the Mediator, Messiah, New Adam and Saviour presented as powerfully, fully and clearly as it is in the Communion Service of the same *Prayer Book*. A careful examination of the eight Eucharistic Prayers in Order One in "contemporary language" reveals that only one, Prayer C, which is based on the *Prayer Book*, possesses the same profound coverage of the saving work of Jesus Christ as that in *The Book of Common Prayer*. And of the Eucharistic Prayers of Order One in traditional language, again only Prayer C truly covers and celebrates the full mediatorial work of the Lord Jesus Christ.

In fact in those services that belong to the period from 1980 we see a deliberate toning down of the emphasis upon the Cross and upon the "full, perfect and sufficient sacrifice, oblation and satisfaction" there offered, even as there is also a reduction of the emphasis upon sin as meriting the wrath of God. This is in part probably because of the desire to make services intelligible, accessible, simple and acceptable. Some would think that an element of "dumbing down" is involved here.[1]

A related question is whether or not the "gender inclusive" translation of the Psalter, which is part of the primary volume of *Common Worship*, actually has the effect of reducing the Christological commitment and content of the Psalms as used in Christian worship. That is, if "Man" is removed then a traditional reference to the new Man, the new Adam, has disappeared. We shall address this matter in Chapter Six.

---

1 For this modern practice see Marva J. Dawn, *Reaching Out without Dumbing Down: A Theology of Worship for the Turn-of-the-Century Worship*, Grand Rapids, 1995.

Closely related to the expression of a full doctrine of the Atonement of Jesus Christ is a full doctrine of the human condition before God, the Judge of all men. The recognition by man of his sin before God is an important element of prayer and worship, for by this recognition, and the accompanying penitence, repentance, faith and receiving of absolution, he praises the justice and the mercy of God. This is an emphasis that is rare today but it is one that those who pray the Psalms regularly are very conscious of. If one compares the statements of human sin in the texts for Morning and Evening Prayer, the Litany and Holy Communion, in *The Book of Common Prayer*, with those in *Common Worship*, one sees very clearly in the latter a definite contracting or minimizing of this doctrine of human sinfulness. For example, in the opening of the Litany of *Common Worship*, the congregation prays for the Persons of the Holy Trinity to "have mercy upon us" whereas in the *Prayer Book* it is to "have mercy upon us" as specifically "miserable sinners". Christians only see themselves as "miserable" (needy, poor in spirit) when they also see the pure holiness of God and the precious blood of Christ, shed for them. In the opening of the Confession in Holy Communion the difference is even more clear for the wording in the *Prayer Book* conveys very clearly that sin is hated by God and extremely offensive to him and therefore there needs to be in man full acknowledgement and rejection of sin, earnest repentance, hearty sorrow, and trusting faith.

Now let us move on to another claim made in the Preface: that "worship itself is a pilgrimage—a journey into the heart of the love of God." The beginning of this journey is specifically related to the Service of Baptism, from which rite we learn: "Baptism marks the beginning of a journey with God which continues for the rest of our lives" and we are "journeying into the fullness of God's love". As we reflect upon this idea of worship as a pilgrimage we recall how many thousands of Christians through history have made visits to holy sites—but ususally to worship when they got there, not to treat the journey itself as worship. That is, the journey, though it was seen as an act of consecration to God, was a preliminary activity directed towards worship as an end.

The reference to pilgrimage also makes us recall those two well-known texts in the New Testament where baptized Christians, who are walking in the way of Christ, are called pilgrims:

> These [Abel, Enoch, Noah, Abraham, Isaac and Jacob] all died in faith, not having received the promises, but having seen them afar off, and were persuaded of them, and embraced them, and confessed that they were strangers and pilgrims on the earth. (Hebrews 11:13)

> Dearly beloved, I beseech you as strangers and pilgrims, abstain
> from fleshly lusts, which war against the soul. (1 Peter 2:11)

Here again, worship does not seem to be specifically connected to
pilgrimage, except in the sense that the patriarchs as they travelled
built altars here and there in order to worship at them, and New
Testament Christians met together each Lord's Day, and in some
cases daily, for worship.

If we positively link the theme of pilgrimage with worship, the definition of worship is no longer reasonably restricted to public or private
acts of praise, thanksgiving, intercession and petition, but is applied to
the whole of the Christian life, which is seen as an ongoing journey
"with God" and "into the fullness of God's love". In the Service of
Baptism parents and godparents of children are told that "in baptism
these children begin their journey of faith" and the newly baptized
are told that "in Baptism God invites you on a life-long journey."

Obviously there can be a practical gain in making use of the image
of pilgrimage as long as it is made clear that there is a goal to the
pilgrimage and that this goal includes the perfect worshipping of the
Father through the Son with the Holy Ghost when pilgrims take
their rest in the fullness of the kingdom of heaven of the age to come.

It is easy to discern why the image of pilgrimage is made so
prominent and is so closely integrated with worship if one looks at
the volume with the title *Common Worship: Initiation Services*. Here, as
we shall in Chapter Nine, baptism is related to "faith and process"
and we are told that "there needs to be a healthy interaction between
three aspects of the Christian life: journey, story and pattern." The
traditional themes and ceremonies of the service of Baptism contain
other images that are perhaps more prominent than pilgrimage. The
thought of Christians as disciples and soldiers of Christ comes into
focus when the sign of the cross is made on the forehead of the
candidates: "Do not be ashamed to confess the faith of Christ
crucified. Fight valiantly as a disciple of Christ against sin, the world
and the devil, and remain faithful to Christ to the end of your life."
The model of union with Christ and thus adoption as children of
God arises in the dramatic association of baptism with the death,
burial and resurrection of Christ. The giving of a lighted candle
points to the baptized shining as lights for Christ in the world of
darkness. And so on.[1]

One possible reason for the elevation of the model of pilgrimage
and of its being associated with worship may be that the theme of
pilgrimage is very popular in modern "spirituality" where there is
much emphasis upon what it is to be a pilgrim but, regrettably,

1 On the over-use of the image of *journeying* see also above, pp. 17–18 and below,
pp. 86–7 and 98–9.

virtually nothing on where the pilgrim is going and what is the goal of all the effort! Another may be the notion popular with some liturgists (as we noted in chapter one) that liturgical worship is dynamic rather than static, unfolds in stages, and moves from gathering or assembly through transformation (by Word and Sacrament) to sending out (*missio*).

From the discussion of the pilgrim nature of worship, let us move on to reflect upon that which occurs in worship. Certainly, as the last sentence of the Preface puts the matter, the ideal situation is when worship can "become the living sacrifice of ourselves to the God whose majesty is beyond compare and whose truth is from everlasting". Earlier in the Preface it is claimed (with somewhat less clarity) that "in the worship of God the full meaning and beauty of our humanity is consummated and our lives are opened to the promise God makes for all creation—to transform and renew it in love and goodness." This certainly sounds great, but what does it mean and where can one see this happening before our eyes? If the basic reference "to transform and renew" creation points to the *eschaton*, the end of this world and the arrival and entrance of the kingdom of God of the age to come, then possibly what is here being claimed is that in the Eucharist a vision is afforded and a taste provided of this new heaven and earth, this new epoch and age of the everlasting kingdom of love and goodness. Perhaps, however, such an interpretation is too traditional for *Common Worship*. It seems more likely that what is here being affirmed in an imprecise way is a theology of ecology and the right use of God's good world, both of which are focused in a true Eucharist.

It is possible that the answer to our problem is found in *New Patterns for Worship* (2002) from the Liturgical Commission in the special provisions with the title "God in creation".[1] However, it seems that nothing here actually expresses in prayers and services "the full meaning and beauty of humanity … ". In fact, after an examination of all the contents of all the published volumes of *Common Worship*, no text has been discovered which expands and illustrates the meaning clearly.

Now, in our search for clarity as to what is worship we turn to the first service in *Common Worship* entitled, "A Service of the Word", which is not a Liturgy or Rite as such but is rather the outline for one (in fact for innumerable ones), based upon "a common structure". In the instructions as to how to create this "Service of the Word" there are comments and observations made about worship

---

1 G25, G61, G62, G 63, G.66, Harvest [16] and All Creation worships [22]—see also B42 and F47, 48, 49.

which we need to examine for they possibly include vital clues not found in the Preface as to what worship is.

"It is important," we are told,

> that those who prepare for and take part in A Service of the Word should have a clear understanding of the nature of worship and of how the component parts of this service work together. Leading people in worship is leading people into mystery, into the unknown and yet the familiar. ... The primary object in the careful planning and leading of the service is the spiritual direction which enables the whole congregation to come into the presence of God to give him glory.

Leaders are required to have both a "clear understanding of the nature of worship" (the essence or true being of worship) and the inter-relation of the component parts (the content within the structure). But as yet we have not been told precisely what is the nature of worship, and apparently nowhere in *Common Worship* is there a succinct definition of worship. Hints are dropped here and there but in the main it seems to be assumed that those using these services will have an idea of what worship is that needs no clarification. It is interesting to recall that when *The Alternative Service Book 1980* appeared, one of the guides to it, *Anglican Worship Today* (edited by Colin Buchanan *et al.*), began with two chapters on the nature of worship. In 1980 it was deemed necessary to tell us what worship is. Perhaps we are to assume that what we were told in 1980 applies in 2000 and afterwards?

In relation to *Common Worship* one of the hints made is the claim that leading people into worship is actually "leading people into mystery, into the unknown and yet the familiar". Then we are told that worship is or includes "the whole congregation coming into the presence of God to give him glory". We may affirm that the Holy Trinity is a Mystery at least in the sense that the Triune God, who creates in us a profound sense of awe, dread and wonder, is beyond our comprehension. He draws us towards himself magnetically and yet we are simultaneously repelled by his glorious and pure holiness. He is like a tremendous fire the sight of which causes us to want to get close and observe; but, at the same time the powerful heat and light drive us back. Thus at times we experience "the sense of the Numinous" as Rudolph Otto described it in his influential book, *The Idea of the Holy*.

But perhaps what is intended here in "A Service of the Word", which can also become "A Service of the Word with a Celebration of Holy Communion", is that by the use of the familiar (e. g., bread and wine and water, incense and candles, chanting and singing) a congregation is led into a mystical and sacramental union with God the Father through Jesus Christ and by the activity of the Holy Spirit. However, in contrast to the *Prayer Book*, where the fear of God, holy reverence and dread before him are highly emphasized and prized as ingredients of spiritual worship, in most texts of *Common Worship* this emphasis is not obvious. Rather, God's welcome and our feeling relaxed and comfortable in the divine presence seem to be suggested. And to "give glory to God", while being obviously related to such things as the Gloria, is also practically speaking often associated with hearty singing and a strong communal feeling of togetherness.

In the chapter on "A Service of the Word" in *A Companion to Common Worship* we are given a further hint as to what worship is:

> So the choice of which words and texts are used is only part of the required preparation. Equally important are the vision of what worship is, the use of the worship space, colour and symbol, and the structure, shape, flow and action in the service.[1]

Here we are told that our vision of what is worship, how we use and decorate the holy place for worship and the overall structure/shape and movement of the service, are all together just as important as is the verbal content in texts used. All this is reasonably clear except perhaps the clause "the vision of what worship is". This suggests that there are several or many possible visions and that having one of these in mind will affect the way that the service is planned and executed and the holy place organized and decorated. One vision could be that of people in togetherness drawing near to God and in unison singing and speaking before him. The "worship space" would be organized to symbolize this with, for example, the chairs set in the round and the walls covered with posters indicating cooperation, community, fellowship and togetherness. Another rather different vision could be that of the church as a hospital for sick sinners thanking God for his healing power and asking for his forgiveness for the sins that have caused the sickness. Here the emphasis would be on the "vertical" relation with God and thus signs of his transcendence and of his mercy, together with manifestations of human penitence and thankfulness, would be prominent.

The Church as a whole can accept a "vision of worship" and from this produce a common text with common ritual and ceremonial to be used everywhere (allowing of course for some local adaptation and input) and such is what is found in *The Book of Common Prayer* and the Service Books of the Orthodox Churches. Or the Church can allow all her individual parishes to develop a local "vision of worship" and adapt publicly available prayers, praises, creeds and

1 p. 61

structures to express the local vision. Unless all the local parishes are very well instructed in the Catholic Faith the method of following the local vision (which in practice usually means the vision of one or two dominant personalities) runs the real danger of both excessive dumbing down and allowing into the churches, perhaps unwittingly and sincerely, all the ancient heresies along with new ones, dressed in the respectable clothing of "common worship".

In *New Patterns for Worship* (2002) the Liturgical Commission recommends that before services are constructed there be local discussion as to what is worship[1] and to get the talking started provides some definitions which seem to have the approval of their writers. They are:

> Worship is a door open in heaven. We lift up our hearts, listen to what God is saying, join the angels and archangels and all the saints in heaven in praising God's eternal holiness. We are there and he is here.
> Worship is a door open to the inner depths of life. Suddenly, as we worship, wholeness, shalom, peace, come to us as all the fragmented bits of our being are put into God's perspective. Things make sense, and there is something to hold on to which has hitherto seemed just beyond the grasp of our mind.
> Worship is a door open to the rhythms of life. Through festivals, simple rituals, a weekly rhythm, worship marking morning and evening, the whole of life, time and space is claimed for God and given back to him. In the worship he gives it to us again, to use for him, and we know he is concerned with our hopes and fears, politics and problems, families and finance.
> Worship is a door to our hearts open in obedience to God. He commands us to worship in spirit and in truth. We respond to the overwhelming majesty of his beauty revealed in creation, to his overwhelming love and grace revealed in his word and in his Son. And as we worship, we are changed.[1]

In this thought-provoking presentation, worship is presented as a door that is open in heaven, to the inner depths of our lives, to the rhythms of life, and to obedience of God. But the use of the picture or image of the door is not immediately helpful since whatever worship is, it is activity (spiritual, moral, mental, physical, individual and communal) by certain human beings addressed to another unique Being, the Lord God, who is beyond infinity and eternity. Though a door swings open, it hardly represents the total personal action of a human being or of an assembly of human beings. Possibly what is meant is that worship occurs when these various doors are opened by the Holy Spirit or our preparation or both.

---

1 pp. 26ff.

Now let us move on to consider the actual content of prayers, and in particular some collects. It must be acknowledged that what we referred to above as a "dumbing down" is widespread in modern popular services of worship in the West, as we descend to the lowest possible common denominator to ensure that all present can follow what is going on. This phenomenon is to be seen in much of the results of "the church growth movement" in various parts of the world, America and Korea for example. At the same time it must also be stated that "dumbing down" is not a necessary consequence of using new liturgy and so-called "contemporary language". This agreed, it probably can be fairly adduced against the Church of England that her very latest collection of *Additional Collects*,[1] which was first brought to the General Synod in February 2003 and as I write awaits final approval, is susceptible to the charge of "dumbing down". It is intended as a supplement and thus an alternative to the collection already in use and entitled, "Collects and Post-Communions for Sundays, Principal Holy Days and Festivals".

This primary collection of Collects in *Common Worship*, which are provided in both contemporary and traditional language, is not perfect; and later on in this book we shall have reason to offer some critical comments of content and style. However, this criticism will not be primarily about "dumbing down", which applies specifically to the 2003 collection. The consultation exercise undertaken by the Liturgical Commission before the writing of the new simplified prayers produced a wide range of criticisms of the present collects in *Common Worship* and some of these criticisms we shall notice in chapter nine.

It is appropriate to examine several of the results of this process of simplification. Here are three in a row of the new collects:

> *Christmas Eve*
>
> Almighty God,
> as we prepare with joy
> to celebrate the gift of the Christ-child,
> embrace the earth with your glory
> and be for us a living hope
> in Jesus Christ our Lord

> *Christmas Night*
>
> Eternal God,
> in the stillness of this night
> your almighty Word leapt down from heaven:
> pierce the world's darkness with the light of salvation
> and give to the earth the peace that we long for
> through our Saviour, Jesus Christ.

---

1 *Common Worship: Additional Collects* GS 1495, 2003

Christmas Day

Lord Jesus Christ,
your birth at Bethlehem
draws us to kneel in wonder at heaven here on earth:
accept our heartfelt praise,
as we worship you,
our Saviour and our eternal God.

They are certainly brief; each is one sentence, though two of them make use of the colon to separate the giving of information from the petition.

The first one uses the popular but hardly biblical expression "Christ-child". Further, unless previously told or in the know one would not necessarily associate "the Christ-child" of line 3 with "Jesus Christ our Lord" of the last line. The former could be the offspring of the latter! Then, what "embrace the earth with your glory" means is far from clear, even though it may sound good.

In the second, the "Eternal God" is informed that his almighty Word leapt down from heaven. Whatever be the aptness of this dramatic metaphorical picture, it cannot point to any basic biblical truth because the Word had already taken to himself in the womb of the Blessed Virgin Mary his humanity as from 25 March and was thus already present as One Person with two natures in the womb of Mary, ready to come forth into the world in his own right as the Incarnate Son, Emmanuel.

The third, which is addressed to Jesus, tells him that we are drawn to kneel in wonder at heaven as we exist on earth. Why do we not kneel specifically before the same Lord Jesus for whom heaven exists?

They appear to be written in order primarily to sound good in their brevity when spoken rather than to convey accurate doctrine and clear petition for genuine worshippers.

Ordinary people over the centuries have learned off by heart the Collects from *The Book of Common Prayer* and, whether or not they fully understood the totality of truth within their one sentence, often with a relative clause and a doxology, they appear to have found them meaningful prayers in time of trial and temptation, difficulty and distress, as parish priests who visit their flock have long known. Why we need to simplify them, even for mission congregations, in this day and age remains a puzzle, especially when we can end up not with genuine simplicity but with semi-meaningless expressions.

Worship and the Prayer Book

According to *The Book of Common Prayer*, worship as a public, corporate activity is specifically offered in the Sacrament of Baptism (followed by Confirmation), in the daily Morning and Evening Prayer, and by Morning Prayer, Litany, Holy Communion with sermon and Evening Prayer on the Lord's Day (with similar arrangements for Feast Days). For many parishes which use the *Prayer Book* in the third millennium it must be admitted that for them this is an ideal rather than a norm, for they seem only to be able or ready to manage one or two services on Sundays and an occasional one mid-week. Nevertheless, to understand the meaning and content of worship in the *Prayer Book* one must examine what it presupposes and expects.

The purpose of both Morning and Evening Prayer is contained in the address to the assembled congregation that begins, "Dearly beloved brethren ... ." We hear these words:

> ... when we assemble and meet together to render thanks for the great benefits that we have received at his [God's] hands, to set forth his most worthy praise, to hear his most holy Word, and to ask those things which are requisite and necessary, as well for the body as the soul.

So, thanking, praising and petitioning God, as well as hearing what he has to say to us, are all basic ingredients of this service. But so also is the confession of sins, which is seen not only as a necessary preparation for approaching God—"with a pure heart and humble voice unto the throne of the heavenly grace"—but also as a necessary part of the praise and worship of God. We are to confess our sins "with an humble, lowly, penitent, and obedient heart; to the end that we may obtain forgiveness of the same, by his infinite goodness and mercy". Therefore a General Confession said by all, followed by an Absolution, immediately occurs after this address. It is important to observe that the confession of and the turning away from sins is not presented as something we need to get over quickly so as to move on to the more important activity of "celebration" but as a necessary part of the praise of God. This is because our humble and sincere confessing of sin is also our celebrating his radiant holiness and his merciful forgiveness.

Worship may be described as a primary ingredient of our duty to God. Thus in the Catechism in response to the Question, "What is thy duty towards God?", the answer provided is:

> My duty towards God is to believe in him, to fear him, and to love him, with all my heart, with all my mind, with all my soul,

and with all my strength; to worship him, to give him thanks, to put my whole trust in him, to call upon him, to honour his holy Name and his Word, and to serve him truly all the days of my life.

The spiritual heights of Christian worship are there to be attained in what the Early Church called The Eucharist, entitled "The Order for the Administration of the Lord's Supper or Holy Communion" in the *Prayer Book*. Here the centrality of Jesus Christ as the only Mediator between God and man, the necessity of his unique Atonement, the glory of his bodily Resurrection and Exaltation, and the union of the Church to him by faith through the Holy Ghost are made abundantly clear. "We in him and he in us" is the relation established by God through this Sacrament as the assembly of Christ's flock eat the bread and drink the wine in penitence and faith, in thanksgiving and praise, in the presence of the same exalted Lord Jesus Christ.

Once again in this *Prayer Book* service, the praise of God and union with Christ include the confession of sin and turning away from it. What has been called justification by faith—trusting wholly in the merits of the Christ the Redeemer and repudiating any claims of one's own for peace with God—is certainly a prominent theme, but it is clearly linked to the doctrine of union with Christ. The heavy emphasis on sin (so resented by some modern people) is there to make clear both how abominable it is in God's sight and so to be confessed in humility and penitence, and how great is the mercy of the Holy Trinity which provides for the complete forgiveness, cleansing and removal of sin.

Certainly the Service in the *Prayer Book* of 1662, unlike that in the first *Prayer Book* of 1549, does not conform to the shape or content of the medieval Mass in the Sarum Use. Neither does it conform to the shape or content recommended by Gregory Dix in his influential book *The Shape of the Liturgy*. However, neither of these facts takes away from this Service its profoundly biblical character and shape, together with its ability in the presence of the Holy Ghost to lead those who use it in sincerity and truth from earth to heaven into fruitful union with the Lord Jesus Christ. Testimonies to its fruitful godliness abound from the seventeenth to the twentieth century.

It is the presumption of the *Prayer Book*, and something which Richard Hooker, the Anglican apologist, makes explicit, that common public prayer/worship is superior to private prayer for spiritual and moral efficacy. In Book V of his *Ecclesiastical Polity* Hooker waxes eloquent concerning the beauty, orderliness and efficacy of common prayer in the public place (church). Private prayer should be energised and inspired from the central spring of prayer, public worship, rather than being that from which common prayer has its origin. Finally, much spiritual benefit comes from the discipline of using constantly a fixed text which is theologically sound and memorable.

Summary

One difference between *The Book of Common Prayer* and *Common Worship* is clear to all, that of size. Because of the vast choice built into the latter, it is probably ten times the size of the former! In fact the provision of *Common Worship* is so immense that the only way for a small parish to benefit from it is for there to be a choice made from the variety and for that to become the locally fixed or semi-fixed regular liturgy for Sundays and principal Feasts. However, to make this choice and to be confident that it is a wise one is far from easy. It requires above-average understanding and skill in those who do the choosing. The point is that for there to be right habits of worship present in a parish, there has to be stability and there has to be a liturgy that contains all the basic ingredients of true public worship, even if only a minimal number of options are built into that local liturgy. Then a question will always remain as to whether this under-standing and skill is both present and used.

Another question will also be there in the larger parish (but perhaps not often asked) where an attempt is made to make use of the variety in an "imaginative" way, with different options present each Lord's Day and even on weekdays. It is this: Is it spiritually good for their personal sanctification for some Christian people to have so much power to choose how a congregation worships the Lord our God each Sunday? The wisdom of the centuries points to the great danger of mistaking true freedom in Christ, wherein we submit to his way to find his freedom in us, with a worldly type of freedom where we choose this or that way to serve him and our freedom is in our will. Is not a fairly fixed liturgy better for the sanctification of the people of God and their experience of Christ's service, which is perfect freedom, than a situation where they are choosing something different all the time?

If the result of the Church of England's *Common Worship* as the availability of an ever expanding collection of texts is that each small (even large) parish creates its own "common prayer" through its own fixed and familiar liturgy and thereby uses only a very small part of that which is on offer and available, then the further question arises why was such a massive production necessary in the first place? It seems that the only commonality of worship envisaged in the national Church is that all parishes and cathedrals should use a structure and contents which are wholly available for all in, as it were, the same liturgical supermarket. Further, as there appears to be no consistent doctrine of the nature or essence of worship in the provisions of *Common Worship*, but only hints as to what it may be, it is more than likely that the services in use, and the local ceremonial and music, will provide a veritable assortment of views as to who is God, what is celebration, and how God is worshipped. As time goes by it may well be increasingly difficult to have meaningful diocesan, deanery and joint services because of the diversity of experiences of worship in a given region.

CHAPTER FOUR

The Eucharist

Already in the chapter on Worship we have taken a preliminary look
at the varied and detailed provisions for the celebration of the
Eucharist in *Common Worship*. Here we shall consider in more detail
the shape, content and doctrine of the variety of texts for the Holy
Communion presented within Order One and Order Two. There will
be no detailed consideration of the idiom of public prayer used since
the subject of appropriate language for public worship will be taken
up later, in Chapter Ten.

Shape

In the Church of England the example of the Early Church has
always been of great importance for determining not only the
doctrine of the Eucharist but also the ingredients of the service.
Further, the more ancient the source providing the structure,
ingredients and doctrine of this service, the more attention it is given
by scholars. At the same time, as the dogma of the First Four
Ecumenical Councils was always taken most seriously, liturgy
produced in the light of this doctrinal development was treated as
special. This great respect for ancient teaching and practice provided
the context for the excessive influence of Dom Gregory Dix (1901–
52) who had no time for, or patience with, the *Prayer Book*, for he
regarded Anglican liturgy as parenthetical in the history of liturgy.
He described a fourfold "shape" of the Eucharist largely derived
from *The Apostolic Tradition*, a third-century work attributed to
Hippolytus of Rome. In Dix's book *The Shape of the Liturgy* (1945) is
set forth a structure made from the four actions of the taking of the
bread and wine; the thanksgiving; the breaking of bread; and the
giving to the communicants. This shape, with minor refinements, can
be seen in the eucharistic prayers of *The Alternative Service Book 1980*
and particularly the third, which is modelled on it; this influence is
acknowledged, even celebrated, in *A Commentary on The Alternative*

Service Book 1980, page 57, as providing a totally different path from the liturgical revisions of the 1920s.

Those who produced the final form of the eucharistic prayers in *Common Worship* were obviously much concerned with the shape of the whole rite. Indeed the concept of "the shape of the service/rite/ liturgy" seems to be too prominent. A page each of a contents list called "Structure" precedes the two distinct Orders;[1] within the services themselves the various parts have headings printed in large type and, for major divisions, in red italics. However, what the Liturgical Commission did not do, and for this they are to be warmly complimented, was to force the Content of the Service from *The Book of Common Prayer* into the new Shape pioneered in Series 2 and 3 and *The Alternative Service Book 1980* and continued in *Common Worship*.[2] In the USA, the Episcopal Church used the basic content of the classic *Prayer Book* (1928 edition) service but forced it into the shape of the new services (called Rite II) to produce what was called Rite I in the official 1979 *Prayer Book*. The shape of the Eucharist in this 1979 book is basically the same as that in the 1980 English book where the passing of the peace lies in between the ministry of the word and the ministry of the sacrament, and this is so whether it be the traditional language rite or the modern language one.

In the *Common Worship* Order One Eucharist the adherence to the Dix theory of the supposed four-fold action is identified in or around the text itself in both the contemporary or traditional-language versions. We find the "Taking of the Bread and Wine", "The Eucharistic Prayer" [= the Thanksgiving], the "Breaking of the Bread" and the "Giving of Communion".[3] However, in Order Two in either traditional or contemporary language it is the structure of the *Prayer Book* from the Sursum Corda onwards that is followed and in this there is no four-fold action.

Whether this fourfold action is really as obvious or prominent in the ancient rites as Dix claimed is debated, as is also whether or not the action is better described as twofold or threefold. Thus the question arises as to the wisdom of so clearly identifying the fourfold by sub-headings in the texts of the service. Further, we need to face the possibility that "shape" may be a spin-word which sometimes means no more than the inclusion of certain ingredients. It is not clear that the inclusion of the right parts will always make the right shape, if *shape* (as Dix thought) means something with the wholeness of a drama.

There is another use of the word "shape" with regard to the Eucharistic Prayers in *Common Worship*. It relates to the whole Prayer, its content of Praise and Petition. What is called the Western shape is essentially that of the medieval western Church, which was continued

1 See pages 166 and 228.　　2 pp. 166ff.　　3 pp. 175, 176, 179, 180

in *The Book of Common Prayer*, not only in 1549 but also from 1552, but in a distributed or truncated form. This shape is continued in Order One, Prayers A, B, C and E, where the Thanksgiving ends at the Sanctus and the remainder is petitionary, with the Institution narrative set within this. In contrast Prayers D, F, G and H are said to be

> largely patterned after the classic Eastern "Antiochene" shape, in which the praise has a more extended narrative character, telling the story of salvation history to a greater or lesser degree, and the *Sanctus* and institution narrative are both incorporated within that part of the prayer.

To demonstrate the difference between the Western and Eastern shapes, a diagram is provided showing how the Eastern shape has supposedly a greater content of praise.[1]

Reflecting upon this distinction between praise and petition, it is possible to claim that the so-called "petitionary" element actually praises and thanks God just as much as does the narration of God's mighty acts of salvation of the Old and New Testaments. The humble acknowledgement before God, the Father, of what his Son, the Lord Jesus Christ, has done for the salvation of man, is the basis of the petition and the recital of the Institution by the same Jesus Christ. The Western shape, as found in *The Book of Common Prayer*, presupposes thankful, humbled and praising hearts in the powerful and evocative relative clauses,

> who of thy tender mercy didst give thine only Son Jesus Christ to suffer death upon the Cross for our redemption; who made there ... a full, perfect, and sufficient sacrifice, oblation, and satisfaction, for the sins of the whole world ... .

Here the purpose of the skilful use of the *Deus qui* (God, who) in the relative clause is with appropriate reverence and godly fear to remember before God aspects of his nature, character, attributes or mighty deeds, in order to be in the right frame of mind and piety of heart to make petition of him.

Shape, we must note, is foundational for "A Service of the Word with a Celebration of Holy Communion",[2] since there is *nothing but* "shape" in the presentation of this "service". The content of the listed ingredients is supplied by material from elsewhere, whether from *Common Worship* or composed for the occasion. It is interesting to note that a similar provision is found in the American Prayer Book of 1979.[3] This has commonly been described in recent days as "the hermeneutical key" to the whole Prayer Book, for, it is claimed, it makes clear that liturgy is more than a text and emphasises that it is

1 *Companion to Common Worship*, pp. 138, 139
2 *Common Worship*, p. 25
3 pp. 400–1

communal action. This kind of claim is important for various reasons and of these the ecumenical is perhaps the most obvious. The Episcopal Church is now in full communion with the Evangelical Lutheran Church and the claim that the shape is primary makes inter-communion that much easier, for Lutherans have never had the equivalent of *The Book of Common Prayer* as both Text and Formulary. They have never had Liturgical Formularies to unite them as a juris-diction of the Church of God. Rather they have been a Confessional Church ("We believe, teach and confess ... ") based upon the Augsburg Confession, and the structure of their worship has been guided in principle not by a common text but by common structures. Their Liturgical Books are not primarily collections of texts but essays on how to lead liturgy and teach the Faith. Many Lutheran parishes have used common services, but for them common prayer means not a common text but a common (and minimal) structure for Word and Sacrament. Perhaps this provision of shape only in *Common Worship* will be hailed also as "the hermeneutical key" to the Eucharist, especially since the Church of England has various agreements with Lutheran State Churches in Europe.

In *New Patterns for Worship*, the Liturgical Commission provides a set of rules and an abundance of advice concerning "planning and preparing Holy Communion".[1] Various examples of A Service of Holy Communion, constructed within the terms of reference provided in *Common Worship*[2] are supplied, including a special one on "All Creation Worships".[3] Those who embark on this exercise have so much to bear in mind and so many choices to make that to produce something satisfactory as a means of worshipping the Holy, Blessed and Undivided Trinity is to say the least very difficult, and the most, virtually impossible.

The Gathering

In Order One, the first part is called "The Gathering", followed by "the Liturgy of the Word". The parts which make up "the Gathering" are: Greeting, Prayer of Preparation, Prayers of Penitence, Summary of the Law, Invitation to Confession, Confession, Kyries, Absolution, Gloria in Excelsis and the Collect. While "the Gathering" may include most of these parts, the only required ones appear to be the opening "Greeting" and the Collect of the Day. Confession seems to be optional. It is important to observe two things here. First, that this is the only place in Order One where it is possible to make confession of sins and hear the divine word of forgiveness, unless one reckons that this is achieved by the Lord's Prayer. Secondly, that

1 pp. 21ff.   2 p. 25   3 pp. 458ff.

because confession of sins is placed in what is often termed "the preparation" it is not linked distinctly and directly, as it is in Scripture and in the *Prayer Book*, with the praise of God and true worship of him. It has been the tendency in modern times to treat the confession of sins as that which we need to get out of the way as efficiently as possible in order to get to the real business of celebration. In contrast in *The Book of Common Prayer* the Collect for Purity and the recital of the Ten Commandments are compulsory and the confession and absolution, which come later in the service, are also a necessary part of the spirituality and doctrine of the service.

In some modern Anglican high church traditions it is the custom to have no public confession or absolution in the Liturgy in "the great fifty days of Easter" and also the period from Christmas to Epiphany. This kind of thing seems to be permitted by the rubrics of Order One. Again in contrast to this, the *Prayer Book* reckons us to be sinners for 365 days a year and in high and low seasons and thus we are always in need of divine cleansing, and as such, we need to praise the justice of God which condemns our sins and the mercy of God that forgives us as we appear before him in penitence and humility seeking remission and forgiveness.

"The Greeting" in Order One contains as an option: "The Lord be with you" from the minister with the response "And also with you" from the whole congregation. In the *Prayer Book* (and in Order Two, following the *Prayer Book*) the response made by the whole congregation is "And with thy spirit." Thus one would have expected, "And with your spirit," in modern renderings. However, this ancient exchange has been made to sound like, and is now called, a Greeting. It was rendered into a modern paraphrase (initially by the International Consultation on English Texts, 1970) and has appeared in prayer books/liturgy, e. g., the ECUSA 1979 *Prayer Book*, in this "greeting" form for thirty years or so now. But, as used in church, this exchange is not a simple greeting as if to friends in the street or at the club. It is a profound dialogue wherein the presence of the Lord Jesus by his Spirit is being humbly claimed, affirmed and accepted in general terms and also being asked for in specific terms.

The traditional English form is a direct, literal translation of the original Latin, long used in the Church in western Europe:

> Priest: *Dominus vobiscum.*
> People: *Et cum spiritu tuo.*

Here the first line has the second person plural—*you*, i.e., the members of the congregation, while the second line has the second person singular—thou/*thy*, the Minister/Priest.

And this Latin form of the exchange and dialogue was/is used in both the Daily Services of the Church and the Mass. The rubrics allowed this exchange to be only between Bishop or Priest and congregation in the Mass and between Bishop, Priest or Deacon and congregation (if any) in the Daily Offices. That is, the congregation were not to say, *et cum spiritu tuo*, to a subdeacon or to a lay reader.

The meaning of "The Lord be with you" is reasonably straightforward. The Minister addresses the people and claims the promises of the Lord Jesus, which he made to his disciples, for example, "Where two or three are gathered together in my Name there am I in the midst of them" (Matthew 18:20) and "I am with you always even unto the end of the world" (Matthew 28:20). Christ is with them especially when as the Body of Christ and Household of God they meet at his Table on his Day to celebrate his Resurrection and to feast at his Banquet. Though the Lord Jesus has ascended into heaven, he is present with his people in and through the Holy Ghost, who is called by St Paul, the Spirit of Christ.

The meaning of "and with thy spirit" is also reasonably straightforward—or at least it used to be. It is addressed by the congregation to the Minister and is first of all the recognition that he has been ordained to serve the Lord in his Church and to minister amongst and to this gathered people. At ordination a spiritual gift from the Lord Christ was given unto him and it is in direct reference to this that the congregation says, "and with thy spirit". It is thus a confident prayer that the ordained Minister will conduct the service as one who is inspired by and guided by the Spirit of the Lord according to the spiritual gift, a gift from the Lord Christ through the Holy Ghost, bestowed upon him at ordination. Thus "spirit" here refers both to the Holy Ghost and to the human spirit to which is grafted or united the spiritual gift of ordination. It is an expression of humble confidence by the congregation that the divine worship will be an encounter with the Lord Jesus in spirit and in truth through the ministrations of his ordained servant. The decision to replace *et cum spiritu tuo* with "And also with you" removes this reference to the particular status, role and calling of the ordained Minister and his place and purpose at the Eucharist. It makes him merely the leader of the group (or presider at the assembly). We may thus claim that the use of "And also with you" is a great loss to the full, historic and traditional meaning of worship and of ordination in the Catholic Church.

We recall that the modern translation has been justified on the basis that the original expression was a Semitism—that it was used in Palestine in Aramaic as a greeting. Now, even if this is true, the fact remains that it took on a specific theological and liturgical meaning in the Early Church when they gathered for the Eucharist with their bishop. And that meaning became the true meaning for Christians. In other words, "and with thy spirit" may have begun its journey as an everyday greeting outside the Church, but it is transformed by its use in divine service and in its use at a meal that is unlike any other meal, the Eucharist. We do no service to the cause of truth by avoiding the meaning that it has in all the texts and teaching of the Early Church with respect to the Eucharist. Happily, the Vatican is now—at last—requiring those who produce English texts for the Church to translate, "And with your spirit". We may consider that this is good and right, for it was the misplaced zeal of RC translators in the 1960s/1970s that introduced us all to the strange expression (hardly modern English) "And also with you," and thereby cut us off from a sound tradition of doctrine.

Perhaps this is a good place to make a comment on the name given to the bishop or priest or minister in this service, the name of "the president". There are obvious attractions to the use of this word, since it can refer to both female and male clergy. However, it is somewhat dated, for the right title now seems to be "the presider" to convey a sense of action and drama in the service. The claim that this name is an ancient, pre-Constantinian title for the bishop or priest who celebrated the Eucharist is not based on such a sure foundation as often supposed. In *The Apology* of Justin Martyr, the bishop or head of the college of presbyters is called "the president of the brethren" and then later this is shortened to "the president." But the meaning of *president* is to be gained not from its standing alone but with "of the brethren". It would seem a better practice to use the title of "Celebrant" or "Minister". Further, "president" will soon become "presider" as in much of the recent provision of the American Episcopal Church.

Liturgy of the Word

In this section are three Bible readings, a Creed and Prayers of Intercession. We shall only examine the Creed here, leaving reflections upon the Bible and Prayer to Chapters Eight and Nine.

The Nicene Creed is to be used on Sundays and Holy Days. In the Church of England there are two authorized translations, that in *Common Worship* and that in *The Book of Common Prayer*. These are obviously different. Here are some of the issues raised when the two are compared.

The first question is whether to begin "I believe" or "We believe". The claim made by those who first provided the plural form in the 1970s was that in the documents of the Ecumenical Councils of the Church from 325 to 451 the text begins in the plural in both the Greek and the Latin versions. The Bishops there assembled said in unison, "We believe ... ." So far they are entirely right. Next, they said, we should therefore follow the Councils and use the plural, for that form is the most authentic and original. Here they began to go wrong. Why? Because the Creed we know as the Nicene Creed was taken by the bishops to their churches and used as the baptismal Creed (especially in the East) and as such they changed it to the first person singular, *I believe*. When eventually the Nicene Creed entered the Liturgy it entered as the baptismal Creed and thus in the first person singular. In the ancient Liturgies of the East and the West it is always and only in the singular. Thus the widespread use of the word, *Credo* (Latin for "I believe"). All the musical settings for the Creed through the centuries are for "I believe" and apparently there are very few examples over the centuries of the plural form of the Creed used in worship, that is until we arrive at the 1970s. It is obvious that "I believe" is the correct form for not only is it the confession of faith of each member of the Body of Christ, it is also the whole Body, the one Body, saying to its Head and Master, "I believe".

In the second place, the question arises of how to refer to the created order. The modern has "all that is, seen and unseen"; the *Prayer Book* "all things visible and invisible". We usually use the word "unseen" to refer to something that is hidden from our eyes or covered so as not to be seen. In contrast we usually use the word "invisible" to refer to something that by its nature cannot be seen— e. g., the wind and the human spirit and mind. The words in the original Greek of the Creed are taken from the New Testament, Colossians 1: 16, "For in Christ all things were created, in heaven and on earth, visible and invisible [Gk, *ta horata* and *ta aorata*]"; and it is of great interest that the New Revised Standard Version of the Bible, favoured by the Liturgical Commission, translates the Greek as "visible and invisible". Since the reference in the Creed is to God's heaven where are the angels, the better word is "invisible" for we cannot by our mortal eyes see this realm and sphere.

Thirdly, the expression "eternally begotten of the Father" is mislead-ing, for it seems to suggest that the Son of God is perpetually and continually being begotten by the Father. The truth being conveyed by the Creed in both its Latin and Greek originals is that the begetting occurred before ages and worlds, that is, out of time. The *Prayer Book* has "begotten of his Father before all worlds", which translates the Latin, "ex patre natum ante omnia saecula". The Greek is "ton ex tou patros gennethenta pro panton ton aionon" which is best translated "begotten from the Father before all ages". Thus the *Prayer Book* version is to be preferred for though it will always need explanation it is nearer to the originals than the modern version. The concept of eternally begetting, being brought into being all the time, is hardly intelligible.

In the fourth place, the phrase "of one Being with the Father" is intended to be a better translation than "being of one substance with the Father". The original Greek contains the famous *homoousios* which had traditionally been translated in English as "the same [= identical] substance", pointing to the divinity of the Son being exactly and wholly the same divinity as the Father. The danger of the new translation in rendering *ousia* as "Being" and thus *homoousios* as "one Being" is that Being may be understood as *a* Being, a Something that is Someone, and thus God is seen as One Being with three primary Names, the Father, the Son and the Holy Spirit. It would have been far better to retain the traditional translation and then explain it to catechumens and confirmands.

Fifthly, the statement "for us and for our salvation he [the Son] came down from heaven, was incarnate from the Holy Spirit and the Virgin Mary and was made man" differs from the *Prayer Book* where *Common Worship's* "for us" is rendered "for us men". This is better, because the idea is that the Incarnation is for the whole human race and not merely and only for the church members of any one time. The reason for the omitting of "men" (Greek original, *anthropos*; Latin, *homo*) is of course the desire to be gender inclusive. Yet here submission to a modern ideology has created false doctrine, serious false doctrine, by changing the purpose of the Incarnation and saving work of the Son of God in restricting it only to "us", which will ordinarily be understood as "church members", rather than as "human beings". Moving on to the second half of this statement we note that in the *Prayer Book* it is rendered "was incarnate by the Holy Ghost of the Virgin Mary". This old translation follows the Latin text in making a distinction by the use of different prepositions, "by" and "of", between the different roles of the Holy Ghost and the Virgin Mary in the act whereby Jesus was conceived. The modern translation follows the Greek text by using twice the same preposition, but in so doing blurs the distinctive role of God and Mary in the assumption by the eternal Son of our human nature in her womb.

Two comments bring this section to a close. First, the Order Two in contemporary language, which is intended to be the *Prayer Book* service rendered into modern English, does not present the Creed in the "I believe" form. Rather it uses the modern form of "We believe" from Order One! Secondly, while the Creed printed in the Liturgy of the Word contains the *filioque* ("and from the Son") and thus rightly presents the official doctrine of the Church of England concerning the procession of the Holy Ghost, a version of the Creed on page 140 which "may be used on suitable ecumenical occasions" is without the *filioque*. Thus it seems the Church of England is of two minds on this doctrine which has divided East and West for a long time. What do we believe? On some occasions one thing and on others another. The suggestion must be that precision in credal formulations is not very important.

The Eucharistic Prayer

After the Gathering or the Preparation comes the Liturgy of the Word, and this is followed by the Liturgy of the Sacrament. The latter may begin with "The Peace".

The source of this activity is said to be the Early Church, which developed it from the "kiss of peace" in the New Testament. A variety of explanations is offered by liturgists as to what was its purpose in the third century and an even greater variety as to what it is meant to achieve in the modern age.

Whatever be its real meaning and purpose, the effect of "the passing of the peace" in some, perhaps too many, churches is to create a major activity between the ministry of the Word and the ministry of the Sacrament, and in some cases, where it is pursued with enthusiasm and major congregational involvement, to make it seem the most important thing in the whole service—the divine sandwich-filling. Thus the the all-important Shape of the service has the feel and the appearance of a sandwich. In fact the Peace has been dubbed "the sacrament of panentheism" in situations where its nature, noise and activity seem excessive.

Perhaps there are some places and services wherein the Peace does achieve what the word suggests, peace and reconciliation between those at enmity and thus peace with God and one another before approaching the altar (see Matthew 5:23–4). But bearing in mind how open this activity is to abuse (e. g., men searching out pretty females) there is much to be said for using the rubrical provision[1] and either leaving out the Peace altogether or saying the Peace at another place, where there cannot be a general walk-about and hugging. Too much external greeting, as if meeting loved ones at the gate in the airport after a long absence, can also distort the sense of the doctrine of God, making him to be as it were only the God of the horizontal and of feeling, and not the God of transcendence and contemplation.

The Eucharistic Prayer begins with the Sursum Corda, where we immediately note the "and also with you" instead of "and with your spirit". If ever the right translation, "thy/your spirit", is needed, it is here at the beginning of the important address to the Father in the name of his Son and with the Holy Ghost. Further, another example of the commitment to gender inclusiveness occurs when the

1 See page 333.

congregation responds to the Celebrant by saying, " It is right to give thanks and praise". Yes it is, but to whom? *The Alternative Service Book 1980* had "to give him thanks and praise". Is not Jesus the Christ a male and thus is it not right to use "him" with reference to this unique Man?

When we read through the provision of ten versions of "the Eucharistic Prayer" in Order One and two in Order Two and compare them one with another, it is difficult to understand why so many were thought necessary, even though there was a desire to make use of the western and eastern shapes of the Prayer. It is like sitting down for breakfast and having the table in front of you filled with boxes of different cereals which, however, have a basic similarity, so that choice is hard to make! It seems that the variety that characterizes the affluent West in terms of what may be purchased in shopping mall and supermarket has so become part of our general expectations that we need not only the provision of multiple prayers for the Eucharist but also a structure or shape that can be used to create our own local eucharistic prayer. Thus the diversity is in principle extremely great and wide.

In practice, it appears that many parishes choose one of the options, print it as a leaflet, and effectively forget about all the other possibilities, until they get a new vicar or until the Bishop comes along and tells them to try another one. The desire for some standard or regular form at the parish level (where there are usually no liturgists who are excited by all the different possibilities) is wholly understandable. In order to settle down and concentrate and know what is coming next the average worshipper needs to be reasonably familiar with a rite. At best, he needs to be able to learn it by heart.

We recall that the early Church fairly quickly standardized its central liturgical texts (according to rite) as soon as it reasonably could after the Council of Nicea (325). Thus the eucharistic canons became standard, two in the Byzantine rite, one in the Roman rite, a number, but still set, in the Coptic rite, and so on. Like the standardization of the creed and of doctrinal statements, this was a natural and necessary part of the development of doctrine, both to safeguard orthodoxy and also to ensure the continuity of Holy Tradition.

However, in the *Companion to Common Worship* we are told that

> It is now common in many churches to have more than one eucharistic prayer available for use, each of which has its own distinct emphasis. Rather than trying to say everything in one prayer, they offer a diversity of expressions and scriptural allusions.

So "experiencing and praying at least some of their diversity is generally to be encouraged for all congregations, although certain prayers will be more appropriate for some occasions and situations than others."[1] Perhaps the idea is that there should be the use of at least one in the western shape with one in the eastern shape.

Where are the reasonably simple and clear criteria, whether stated or available, by which a parish priest with the lay leadership can determine which of the options are right for their situation? This need appears not to be addressed in the *Companion*. Indeed in the Foreword the Bishop of Salisbury suggests that we all need to read the book (or the long chapter on the Eucharist) in order to understand sufficiently to make a right choice. Yet practically speaking, decisions seem to be taken—at least in small parishes—on such principles as, what is closest to the use of one of the options from *The Alternative Service Book 1980* with which we are familiar, or which one is like the *Prayer Book* service. The alternatives to the Order for Holy Communion in the *Prayer Book* could have been limited to no more than two Eucharistic Prayers, one Western and one Eastern in shape. And the Outline of the Shape,[2] leaving the content open to local initiatives should not have been made so prominent. By encouraging such an approach to liturgy the Church of England is in danger of losing all sense not only of "Common Prayer" but also of "common doctrine".

In comparing the content of the one, and only one, Prayer of Consecration in the *Prayer Book*, with those of the Eucharistic Prayers in *Common Worship* that are not based on the *Prayer Book*, we shall here note two characteristics of the latter—a studied ambiguity about the presence of Christ in the Sacrament and a weak doctrine of the saving work of the Lord Jesus at Calvary.

It is well known and generally accepted that on matters which were controversial in the sixteenth century *The Book of Common Prayer*, like The Articles of Religion, was clear—e. g., the completeness and sufficiency of the atoning work of Jesus Christ on the Cross, the crucial role of faith in salvation, and the spirituality of sacramental grace. Examples of studied ambiguity occur in seven of the eight Prayers of Order One. The celebrant asks that the bread and wine may "be to us" or "be for us" the body and blood of Christ. This is a return to the phraseology of the *Prayer Book* of 1549 asking that the elements may be in some way or another (though the way is not specified) identified with the Lord's body and blood. In 1549 the use of such wording represented a move away from the medieval, physical doctrine of transubstantiation (that the whole bread

1 pp. 122, 123   2 *Common Worship*, p. 25

becomes truly the whole body of Christ) towards the more spiritual doctrine later expressed in the *Prayer Books* of 1552, 1559, 1604 and 1662. Here the petition is that by receiving the consecrated bread and wine in faith in the Lord Jesus Christ, we may "be partakers" of his body and blood. Of the eight prayers only one retains the classic *Prayer Book* language.

Perhaps it is not unreasonable to note here that *Common Worship* is the first public Liturgy of the Church of England since the sixteenth century to provide by name for the celebration of the medieval festival of transubstantiation, despite the rejection of transubstantiation in Article 28. Corpus Christi is listed in red on page four as "The Day of Thanksgiving for the Institution of Holy Communion" (kept on the Thursday after Trinity Sunday).[1] The Collects provided add to the studied ambiguity, for the Celebrant prays, "Grant us so to reverence the sacred mysteries of your body and blood that we may know within ourselves and show forth in our lives the fruits of your redemption." Here the treatment of the bread and wine with reverence as sacred mysteries suggests some doctrine of a real presence located in, with or around the physical elements, but the suggestion seems intended not to be clear enough to provoke challenge from those who resist the doctrine of transubstantiation.

The Church of England is a reformed Catholic Church, and one characteristic of such a Church is a very clear and full presentation of the reconciling, atoning, saving, redeeming and sanctifying work of the Lord Jesus Christ, particularly in his passion, crucifixion, descent into hades/hell, and exaltation in a resurrection body of glory to heaven at the Father's right hand. This proclamation and teaching is of course closely related to a full doctrine of human sin and a full doctrine of justification by faith. All three doctrines are most clearly set forth in The Order for Holy Communion in the *Prayer Book*. It takes a truly complete Saviour to save man from the totally devastating nature and effects of sin and evil, and the only way that a man can possibly please God is by believing in and trusting wholly the Lord Jesus Christ, the new Adam.

In *Common Worship* the saving work of Jesus Christ is not so much denied as stated with minimum force and power, and often in what is near to a sentimental style. The minimalism is well illustrated by the Acclamation shared by the modern Roman Catholic Rite (because taken from the same source):

> Christ has died:
> Christ is risen:
> Christ will come again.

1 Collects and Post-Communion Prayers are provided on pages 407 and 479, and further notes are found on pages 529, 534 and 563.

So far so good. But, why did he die?—*for our sins*; and why was he raised from the dead?—*for our justification*; and why will he come again—*for our final and full redemption*! This is left unstated.

When we examine the eight Prayers of Order One that are not related to the *Prayer Book* the weak nature of the declaration of the saving work of Jesus Christ is seen. Again it must be emphasised that it is not denied, but by comparison with the *Prayer Book* minimally stated. The death on the Cross is not connected as fully and clearly as it is in the New Testament and *Prayer Book* with the atonement for and expiation of human sin. For example, in Prayer B the Celebrant prays:

> By the power of the Holy Spirit he took flesh;
> as your Son, born of the blessed Virgin,
> he lived on earth and went about among us;
> he opened wide his arms for us on the cross;
> he put an end to death by dying for us;
> and revealed the resurrection by rising to new life;
> so he fulfilled your will and won for you a holy people.

Here we find that the Father is being told what, as the omniscient Father, he well knows and, we may add, knows more accurately than the race of man! Then what God is being told is as much sentimental as doctrinal. It was the soldiers doing their duty who opened his arms wide and nailed them to the wood. Death was not ended at the Cross but will be so after the Last Judgement, where Christ will be Judge. He did not merely reveal the resurrection but he IS the Resurrection. In fact "revealed the resurrection by rising to new life" is tautologous and hardly attractive prose. What needs to be said is that he was really and truly raised in bodily form from the dead, as St Paul declares in 1 Corinthians 15.

If we examine those Prayers which belong to the Eastern "Antiochene" shape the situation is the same. In Prayer F, at the end of the short narrative of the relation of God to man, and after the Sanctus, the Celebrant says: "Lord God ... in the coming of your Son Jesus Christ / you reveal the power of your love / made perfect in our human weakness," and then continues:

> Embracing our humanity,
> Jesus showed us the way of salvation;
> loving us to the end,
> he gave himself to death for us;
> dying for his own,
> he set us free from the bonds of sin,
> that we might rise and reign with him in glory.

What we have here is imprecision and carelessness leading to unclear doctrine. Let us note that the power of the love of God was not made perfect in our human weakness, but in the voluntary humiliation and weakness of the Incarnate Son who suffered for us. Then the expression "embracing our humanity" is far from clear. It sounds as though he wrapped his arms around it. The Nicene Creed and then the Christological Statement of the Council of Chalcedon (451) provide the orthodox doctrine of the Incarnation in precise terms and this wording should provide the norm for liturgists to follow. The only begotten Son of the Father took to himself human nature in its male expression, and made it his very own, and in that assumed humanity brought us salvation. Then this same Jesus, the Son, did not merely show us the way of salvation, he provided the only way of salvation, for he is the way, the truth and the life. While he certainly died for us, specifically he died for our sins according to the Scriptures, said St Paul.

Conclusion

The emphasis on shape as being all-important and the further emphasis that within the shape there can be a choice from a variety of different ingredients has not been good for Eucharistic worship or for those who engage in it. The provision of ten, and in principle hundreds, of different services of Holy Communion, based on a common structure, is excessive. If an alternative is really needed to the service in *The Book of Common Prayer* then why cannot two texts suffice, one in Western and one in Eastern shape? Surely the supermarket of possibilities should not be introduced into the worship of God, especially into the Eucharist, the Sacrament of Unity.

Further, to place an amended version of the *Prayer Book* "Order for Holy Communion" in *Common Worship* as an alternative alongside the other alternatives is seriously to undermine the status of the *Prayer Book* as the primary doctrinal formulary of the Church of England. One understands that to include the text from the *Prayer Book* in its own idiom and in an attempted modern idiom adds to the range and comprehensiveness of *Common Worship*, but at the same time it treats this text as if it were merely like any other text. Over the centuries, small adjustments have been made to the text of the *Prayer Book* (e. g., using the shortened form of the Commandments and adding some catholic devotions) in parish worship and these are so well known that there was no need to create a new service incorporating some of them. *Common Worship* is an alternative to *The Book of Common Prayer* and should not be offered as the all-inclusive collection that embraces everything, including the *Prayer Book* itself.

CHAPTER FIVE

Daily Prayer

From the Jerusalem Chamber of Westminster Abbey in 1645 came *The Directory for the Publick Worship of God, agreed upon by the Assembly of Divines at Westminster, with the assistance of Commissioners from the Church of Scotland.* From Church House, Westminster in 2000, by the authority of the General Synod of the Church of England, came *Common Worship*, in whose first and main volume the first item is in effect a brief Directory for producing "A Service of the Word" and "A Service of the Word with a Celebration of Communion". This provision was followed in 2002 by what in effect is a full-scale Directory for producing non-sacramental and sacramental services, the book entitled *New Patterns for Worship*, made by the Liturgical Commission of the Church of England.

The provision of a Directory, much favoured by the Puritan Presbyterians of Britain as part of the godly ordering of the Church of God, was received by the Church of Scotland in 1645 but rejected by the Church of England when Charles II was restored to the throne in 1660. In the 1980s, as the new concept of "common prayer" as "shape and ingredients" rather than common text gained favour, so the old Presbyterian idea of a "Directory" was taken up again, not this time by Puritans but by Bishops! In the Introduction to *Lent, Holy Week, Easter* (1984) the Liturgical Commission wrote: "We are providing a directory from which choices may be made. We think of this book as a manual to be used with selectivity, sensitivity and imagination." A year later the General Synod Paper entitled, *The Worship of the Church*[1] called for a

> directory with a wealth of resource material including supplementary material for each of the main points in the service where there is room for the individual's own words. The directory would need to set boundaries to the proposed freedom, and points which might be theologically divisive would have to be watched.

(Whether this watching has been possible must be doubted.) In 2000

---

[1] GS 698, 1985

in *Common Worship* the proposed directory, allowing for diversity
within an authorized skeleton structure, was provided in all but
name, and was then developed in great detail in *New Patterns of
Worship* a couple of years later.

Unlike the modern post-1980 directories, which are addressed to
both the parish clergy and lay leaders and presume no theological
education, that of 1645 was addressed specifically to clergy, who were
assumed to be "godly and learned" men, but still men in need of
practical help in the framing and conducting of Divine Worship—
e. g., on how to assemble the congregation, to read the Holy
Scriptures, to offer public prayer, to preach the Word, to administer
the Sacraments, to observe the Lord's Day, to conduct marriages, to
bury the dead, to sing Psalms, and so on. In the final paragraph of
"the Preface" we read of the need for (in modern terms) "common
prayer" or "common worship":

> the general heads [headings], the sense and scope of the prayers,
> and other parts of publick worship, being known to all, there may
> be a consent of all the churches in those things that contain the
> substance of the service and worship of God.

In the *Directory* there is "some help and furniture" to place under the
"general heads" so that each minister

> by meditation, by taking heed to himself and the flock of God
> committed to him, and by wise observing the ways of Divine
> Providence, may be careful to furnish his heart and tongue with
> further or other materials of prayer and exhortation, as shall be
> needful on all occasions.

There is no indication that before committing itself to the
provision of a modern Directory, the Liturgical Commission
engaged in a careful study of the *The Directory for the Publick Worship*
of 1645 and, for example, took its advice on the absolute importance
in public worship of persuading a congregation to see its sin and
sinfulness before God, and confess the same with a humble, penitent
heart, as an essential ingredient of that worship. Then, one has to ask
whether all modern clergy, who are not so well versed in the content
of the Bible and the Doctrines of the Church as were those of earlier
times, and all lay leaders—likewise not so well versed in Scripture as
were heads of families in Puritan times!—in all parishes, are truly able,
in terms of knowledge, piety, ability and time, to construct services
that are worthy to be used for the public worship of God and replace
the services of *The Book of Common Prayer* in the parish church.

We recall that the *Directory* was produced as a substitute for *The
Book of Common Prayer* because the Presbyterians believed that only
that which is commanded or allowed by Holy Scripture should be a

part of a service of Divine Worship. It took the position against which Richard Hooker had so eloquently argued in his eight-volume *Laws of Ecclesiastical Polity*, at the end of the Elizabethan period. Modern Anglican directories are being produced not because the Church of England is adopting and following the profound scripturalism of the English seventeenth-century Puritans but because of the influence of modern culture, wherein is multiple choice in many areas of life, of which the supermarket is the common symbol. It is believed that provision, within certain constraints and limits, must be made for all ages, all tastes and all educational levels, and so the liturgical books—unlike the Presbyterian *Directory*—grow in size and number.

A Service of the Word

It is extremely significant that the first provision of the main volume of *Common Worship* (2000) is "A Service of the Word".[1] This could have been placed after the texts for Morning and Evening Prayer for Sunday and thereby made less prominent but it was deliberately placed first in order to make absolutely clear that Common Prayer is to be understood in terms not of a common text but of a common structure, shape and ingredients. Twenty years earlier, in *The Alternative Service Book 1980*, there was no hint of this dramatic shift. However, in 1989 appeared *Patterns for Worship* from the Liturgical Commission, in order to provide some indication of different ways of doing liturgy and some suggestions to provide greater freedom to enrich or shorten services. The door had now opened to regularize what had been going on in "Family Services" and "All-Age Services" and other forms of experimental liturgy for a long time. It is of interest to note that the title *Patterns for Worship* was only chosen at the last minute. The title was to have been *A Directory of Resources*. In the view of most liturgists,

> this publication represented a major step in the concept [*sic*] of Anglican worship, seeing it as based upon the idea of a recognizable shape in which some elements are mandatory and others optional, rather than upon any necessary and slavish following of set texts.[2]

When authorized in 1999 by the General Synod, "A Service of the Word" was unique as a Church of England service since apart from the basic menu it consists almost entirely of notes and directions. Further, it allows for much local choice and variation within a

---

1 pp. 21–8. Of these pages three are Introduction and two Notes; "A Service of the Word" and "A Service of the Word with a Celebration of Holy Communion" themselves take a page each.

2 *Companion*, p. 60

common structure. The thinking behind this strategy was that the
needs of parishes would be met not by a group of experts in London
producing services but by a new generation of worship leaders
capable of "generating liturgy which is both local and culturally
relevant while still objectively part of the liturgy of the Church as a
whole".[1] So that we may be clear here is a definition of "A Service of
the Word":

> A Service of the Word is an authorized structure, rather than a set
> text, and allows for the development of locally relevant,
> participatory services which are in tune with the culture, society
> and spiritual life of the local church community. It permits
> considerable flexibility and freedom while maintaining the
> principle of Church of England worship being "that which is
> authorized or allowed by Canon".[2]

The five hundred pages of *New Patterns for Worship* (2002), which
is an update of the pioneering *Patterns for Worship* (1989), are devoted
to helping these local worship leaders prepare both "A Service of the
Word" and "A Service of the Word with a Celebration of Holy
Communion". In the section "How to put a service together" we are
provided with the following instructions:

> The first thing to do is to read the authorized introduction to A
> Service of the Word. ... From this you will see that there are
> three main sections, like three tubs into which you are going to
> put the different items in the service; Preparation, The Liturgy of
> the Word, Prayers. Into these tubs you put the ingredients, the
> different items in the service. Add to these a beginning and an
> ending and you have the main outline.
>
> ...
>
> There are four different kinds of ingredients and it is important
> that there is a balance in the way these are used: Word/Prayer/
> Praise/Action. It is a bit like preparing a meal with three courses,
> plus an appetizer at the beginning and coffee at the end. Each
> course has a number of different ingredients, which can be used
> more than once in different combinations in different courses. It
> is worth noting that for the principal service on a Sunday certain
> ingredients, which are otherwise optional, are required: an
> authorized confession and absolution, an authorized creed or
> affirmation of faith, and a sermon.[3]

In communication, especially with respect to divine things, a great
responsibility is placed upon Christian leaders to use illustrations
that heighten rather than lessen reverence and awe before God and
holy things. The danger in this advice is that the very familiarity of

---

1 *Companion*, p. 61   2 *Ibid.* The Canon is B2.
3 *New Patterns for Worship*, p. 15

the illustrations—tubs, menus, ingredients, three-course meals, appetizers and coffee—tends to make the work and the content of divine worship seem ordinary instead of very special, even unique. In simplifying, we must not engage in dumbing down.

It is also rather worrying that there can be services on the Lord's Day, the only ones to which some people come, that (not being the principal service of the day) do not have a proper call to penitence, a confession of sins and an absolution as well as a creed. As we have previously emphasized, the genuine confession of sin(s) to God the Father through Jesus Christ our Saviour is also the praising of God, the Just and Merciful One. Further, the saying of one of the three ancient Creeds of the Church of England is an act wherein the whole congregation responds to God's revelation by telling him that it has received his word, has summarized its central themes, and is now lovingly repeating it before him, as well as to each other, and to any part of the world that is listening in.

The Liturgical Commission recognizes that "leading people in worship is leading people into mystery, into the unknown and yet the familiar." Thus under the heading of "Theme and Direction" it offers this advice:

> Care should be taken to ensure that there is some overall direction, some sense of cohesion, of going somewhere, some development in the congregation's relationship with God, reflected in the service structure. Sometimes this is provided by a clear theme … .

and sometimes not. The leaders are further urged to ask such questions as

> What do we expect to happen to people in this service? What will be the outcomes for Christian growth, education, deepening appreciation of God, experience of him in worship and praise, and in obedience to his word?[1]

If leading people in worship is leading them into mystery, then it is perhaps going too far to give the impression of needing to have everything as programmed as possible both as to choice of content and evaluation of what is achieved. If it is difficult to choose the right theme and ingredients to make the right content, and to get them in order within the right shape or structure, that difficulty is much increased when it is also a requirement to make psychological, educational and devotional judgements about the people who are being catered for. In fact many people, when they realize the great responsibility placed upon them, will probably want to return to the use of a well-used and tried text of a service and then pray that the Holy Ghost will make that familiar service into a gateway to heaven.

1 *New Patterns for Worship*, pp. 15–16

Daily Prayer

The volume entitled *Common Worship: Daily Prayer* (2002) is in fact a preliminary edition and can only be used by the Church until 2004. Then it will be revised in the light of the experience of its use as its users make their views known. However, the Questionnaire printed in this edition has to be returned no later than June 2003, which means that only one year's use will be the basis for revision in the light of experience. A definitive edition—with whatever finality such things can have—is unlikely before 2005. Likewise the *Common Worship: Daily Lectionary* is only authorized until 2004, and to use the content of *Daily Prayer* one needs the *Daily Lectionary*, which is also to be revised in the light of experience.

What is of tremendous importance for us to grasp is that the canonical legitimacy of the multiple provisions of *Daily Prayer* is conferred by their compliance with the provisions of "A Service of the Word", authorised under Canon B2 as an alternative to the Services of Morning and Evening Prayer in *The Book of Common Prayer* (1662).[1] This in part explains why the first service, or rather structure and ingredients for a service, in the whole of the provision of *Common Worship* is "A Service of the Word". It provides the basis for a vast range of possible forms of service.

The strategy behind *Daily Prayer* is in certain ways comprehensive. It is to collect into one volume, and under the general provision and supervision of the General Synod and its *Common Worship*, what previously was (and still is in reality) found in four sources. First, in *The Book of Common Prayer* (Daily Services, Psalter, Occasional Prayers etc.); secondly, in books used for "The Quiet Time" or daily, private devotions; thirdly, in books of family prayers; and fourthly in forms of the traditional catholic Daily Offices for laity. So there are in *Daily Prayer* outlines of services with some required and many suggested ingredients for private, family and church use and for the major seasons of the year. And before these are provided there are all kinds of practical advice on how to use this varied provision. Therefore, anyone using it to its full potential will need to have (as the definitive edition of the future will have) a set of ribbons or markers in order to go from page to page to make use of what has been chosen from what is available and recommended. It is, of course, possible, and will be so in the future, that a parish or group, intimidated or overwhelmed by the sheer volume of choice, can choose its own shape and ingredients and then print them as a booklet for regular Monday to Saturday use.

1 See further the main volume of *Common Worship*, pp. 26 and 816.

Since at the time of the writing of this chapter it is the season of Lent, it makes sense to examine the provisions for Penitence and Lenten Daily Prayer in this volume. First of all, let us look at the "Forms of Penitence" and "Other Penitential Material" on pages 19 to 25 which may be used at virtually any time, though it is recommended that the third form (which contains no absolution) is not to be used at a Principal Service on a Sunday, Festival or Holy Day. There are in all four responsive forms of penitence, of which three contain absolutions; then there are three prayers of confession of sins and two absolutions. It is only in the Confession adapted from the *Prayer Book* and in "contemporary English" beginning, "Almighty and most merciful Father ... ", that there is a clear and obvious recognition before God the Father of both forms of human sinfulness before God. That is, of daily sins of omission ("have left undone") and of commission ("have done") and that which theologians call original sin ("there is no health in us"). In contrast, some of the other Confessions seem to make very light of the enormous offence to God of human sin both by their brevity and by their lack of a vital sense in their wording of the seriousness of human sin as both a spiritual and moral disease and as a practical failure to love God and man perfectly.

For example, one form of confession is supposedly based on Hosea 6, which is an exhortation by the prophet to the people for repentance:

> Lord our God,
> in our sin we have avoided your call.
> Our love for you is like a morning cloud,
> like the dew that goes away early.
> have mercy on us;
> deliver us from judgement;
> bind up our wounds and revive us;
> in Jesus Christ our Lord.[1]

This begins by admitting one failure within our sin, but it is very vague, for it is not clear what call has been avoided. Is it the two great commandments? Then comes the suggestion that our love of God may be short-lived, but the image of the morning cloud and dew makes it more beautiful than alarming. What we then tell God to do for us is disproportionately greater than what we have confessed, for we request four things—mercy, deliverance, binding up and reviving. Perhaps Hosea 6 has to be studied first to appreciate the content and meaning of this confession of sin. But there it is the going forth of the Lord himself that is compared to the arrival of the morning and the latter and former rain.

1 *Daily Prayer*, p. 21

Then also the wording of the five different absolutions in this section presents the forgiveness of sins in what may be described as a weak and tentative form. Each one begins with the word, "May"; for example, "May the God of love and power forgive you and free you from your sins ... ." This approach is to be contrasted with the absolutions in the *Prayer Book*. For example, "Almighty God, our heavenly Father ... have mercy upon you; pardon and deliver you from all your sins ... ,"[1] "He pardoneth and absolveth,"[2] and "By his authority committed to me, I absolve thee from all thy sins ... ."[3]

Common Worship is littered with the verbal form, "may", not only because of its plentiful use in what used to be called "rubrics"—e. g., "silence may be kept" and "the following may be used"—but also in forms of absolution as we have seen. Now of course *may* is used differently when it expresses a possible state of affairs and when it expresses a wish, but the two uses have *uncertainty* in common. There is a diminution of meaning and spiritual effect in the modern form of Absolution when compared with that of the *Prayer Book*. If we believe that the Holy Ghost is present and active, if we believe that the bishop or priest is ordained by God, and his spokesman, and if we believe that words are intended to have meaning and convey power, then the Absolution is God speaking graciously and directly to the penitent soul the word and the blessing of pardon. And the same is true of Blessings.

From practical experience we all know that "God bless you" is a stronger form than "May God bless you". The Blessing given at the end of Holy Communion in the *Prayer Book* is not "May Almighty God ... bless you" but rather "The Blessing of God Almighty ... be amongst you and remain with you always." In the latter case, a linguistic deed is being performed, and the deed is a heavenly action upon earth. While "May" seems to hanker after a blessing, the form, "The Lord bless ... ", comes with illocutionary force![4]

It is sometimes asked: Why is the jussive subjunctive translated with such a decided preference for the English auxiliary "may" form in the new liturgies—both Roman and Anglican? Here are four possible reasons that need not be mutually exclusive. The first is a sense of humility and a wish not to show presumption towards the Almighty (even though this form of words makes the forgiveness being heard by the people sound less certain). The second is the general ignorance and awkwardness of the committees of liturgists who are not usually specialists in language or remarkable for good judgement about style. For some, it appears, the *may* sounds more elegant. The third is the possible egalitarianism of members of these

1 Order for Holy Communion   2 Morning & Evening Prayer   3 Visitation of the Sick
4 The implications of the liturgical use of "may" are elucidated in "The Question of Style" by Ian Robinson in *The Real Common Worship*, edited by Peter Mullen, 2000, pp. 108ff. For "illocutionary" see J. L. Austin, *How to do Things with Words*, Oxford, 1962.

liturgical committees who wish to avoid giving any impression that the priestly office carries with it any special authority or power of absolution not inherent in "the whole people of God". Finally, the fourth possibility is that with the generally lowered sense of consciousness of guilt and sin in church people today, the desire for an absolution which is certain and clear is not so intense as it was in earlier times.

The specific provision for Lent in *Daily Prayer* is "Prayer During the Day in Lent",[1] "Morning Prayer Lent"[2] "Evening Prayer Lent"[3] and Prayers "For Seasonal Use—Lent".[4] In the first of these, to be used at any time of day, the only provision that is traditionally Lenten in content is the requirement to use one of the short readings from the Bible, all of which rightly include calls to what are known as Lenten disciplines, repentance and fasting, for example. The Collect is either to be that of the day or one based on a prayer of Ignatius Loyola. This means that the traditional Anglican Lenten Collect, which is to be said on each day of Lent, and includes the petition, "Create and make in us new and contrite hearts" is not required.

In *Common Worship*, both Morning and Evening Prayer have the same threefold structure—Preparation, The Word of God and Prayers. Within this basic shape there is much freedom with respect to ingredients with abundant use of "may" to indicate choice. Actually required, and not to be omitted, are the first part of the Preparation (Versicles and a form of Blessing of God), a psalm, a Bible reading, the Gospel Canticle (Benedictus), Intercessions, the Collect of the Day or the Lenten Collect, the Lord's Prayer, and the very brief Conclusion. It is difficult to understand why both the Collect of the Day and the Lenten Collect are not required, as in the *Prayer Book*. Of course, within the permitted options, it is possible to use such an appropriate psalm as Psalm 51 and to have Bible readings that speak of penitence, contrition and fasting, but they are not a necessary part of this particular provision for the Forty Days.

It is difficult to ascertain why within the Preparation the Blessing of God (beginning, "Blessed are you ... ") which comes after the familiar versicles ("O Lord, open our lips" etc.) is required and not optional both in the Morning and Evening. Perhaps the answer is that its general structure and content are based on what is provided as a required part of "Daily Prayer" in *Celebrating Common Prayer*, to which *Daily Prayer* is much indebted. Another possibility is that this form of Blessing is a creation of a prominent member of the Liturgical Commission and she or he wanted to see it actually used and so it is so required. One cannot in justice speak of it as a great example of liturgical writing, even though the claim for it is probably

1 *Daily Prayer*, pp. 59–61   2 pp. 209–14   3 pp. 215–20   4 pp. 338–9

that as a form it was used in the ancient Church in the non-monastic morning and evening services. This Blessing comes with a differing content and theological emphases for different times of the Christian Year as well as for Morning and Evening Prayer. Of the two forms of Blessing provided for Lent, it has to be said that they do not have any particularly special or traditional Lenten flavour. The one for Morning Prayer is the shorter and the weaker of the two:

> Blessed are you, God of compassion and mercy,
> to you be praise and glory for ever.
> In the darkness of our sin,
> your light breaks forth like the dawn
> and your healing springs up for deliverance.
> As we rejoice in the gift of your saving help,
> sustain us with your bountiful Spirit
> and open our lips to sing your praise.
> Blessed be God, Father, Son and Holy Spirit:

All   **Blessed be God for ever.**[1]

This Blessing of God begins and ends in the same format as do many others in *Daily Prayer* and as the originals in *Celebrating Common Prayer*. Yet this beginning and ending seem to be theologically incompatible. The first "you" and "God" are apparently referring to the Father whose "bountiful Spirit" is referred to later in the text. The ending (at "sing your praise") contains no "through your Son" or the like, but ends abruptly without the equivalent of the classic Latin "per eundem ... ". But then comes what appears to be a Blessing not of the Father alone but of the Three Persons of the Blessed Trinity. We say "appears to be" because the formula used is a novel one where a colon separates what are meant to be two statements of intended identical or similar meaning. The sense and the effect of this attempt at a Trinitarian statement would be far better and more in line with patristic orthodoxy if the first Blessing ended with a reference to Jesus Christ, the Son and Mediator, as indicated above, and then if the second Blessing were separated from the earlier one by a line and made to read, "Blessed be God the Father, Son and Holy Spirit" with the response in a new sentence and line, "Blessed be God the Holy Trinity for ever" or even "Blessed be God for ever." As it now stands the presentation of the fundamental dogma of the Christian Faith is imprecise; which is worrying, for this formula is used often in *Daily Prayer*. (We shall return to the subject of orthodoxy of expression in Chapter Nine.)

We have to observe that the verbal content of the first Blessing is disappointing in its lack of reference to clear biblical teaching and central Lenten themes. While it speaks of "the darkness of our sin",

---

1 *Daily Prayer*, p. 209

this form of speech lacks the appropriate, Lenten, touch of personal guilt and accountability before God. Likewise, the references to the light of dawn and the healing springs, though perhaps imaginatively attractive, are vague, and while perhaps making us feel good, do little to create penitence, contrition and faith in our souls. Then, we ask, what precisely is "the gift of your saving help"? Is the gift a specific thing or it is a continuing daily donation of grace? And whatever it is, what is its Lenten association?

Now to a final comment about the two Prayers for Lent.[1] The first one is numbered eleven and begins "In penitence and faith let us make our prayer to the Father ... ." However, it is not clear what is the relation between "penitence" and the list of topics for prayer and intercession that follow the introduction. There is no expression of penitence and no prayer for the right keeping of Lent in preparation for the celebration of Easter. The second one, numbered twelve, is a very brief thanksgiving for Jesus Christ and his saving work but makes no reference to his forty days and nights of fasting in the wilderness.

Finally, it will be useful to look at the collects provided for "An Order of Night Prayer" or Compline,[1] a service not provided in the 1662 *Prayer Book* but found in the 1928 English and the 1962 Canadian (1662 revised) *Prayer Books*. There is one collect printed in the service (a traditional prayer in modern language) and further collects are provided as alternatives for each day of the week and for the seasons of the Christian year. A few of these are familiar prayers such as "Lighten our darkness" but several appear to be composed for this volume. So it is not surprising that some are of poor quality, such as that for Lent:

> Almighty God,
> may we, by the prayer and discipline of Lent,
> enter into the mystery of Christ's sufferings;
> that by following in the Way,
> we may come to share in the glory;
> through Jesus Christ our Lord.[2]

This, in poor English style, conveys a view of Lenten discipline similar to that which is found in the stylish Latin Collect for the First Sunday in Lent in the Sarum Missal, and which the English Reformers rejected as not biblical. In translation that Collect begins, "O God who purifiest thy Church by the yearly observance of Lent" and proceeds to assume that if we offer the good work of abstinence to God, he will cause there to be rewards. The point is that in a reformed Catholic Church genuine good works flow from faith working by love and that even the holiest abstinence, physical and spiritual, cannot earn for us anything at all from God. Further, we

1 *Daily Prayer*, pp. 302ff.   2 p. 317

cannot enter into the fellowship or mystery of Christ's sufferings through our prayers and disciplines, since union with Christ Jesus is a distinct work of the Holy Spirit, the Sanctifier.

The Collect for Passiontide appears to be both imperfectly conceived and poorly written:

> Almighty God,
> as we stand at the foot of the cross of your Son,
> help us to see and know your love for us,
> so that in humility, love and joy
> we may place at his feet
> all that we have and all that we are;
> through Jesus Christ our Saviour.[1]

Before the Cross it is surely appropriate to kneel or to lie prostrate in both grief and adoration. If we are to stand during "the great fifty days of Easter" (as modern liturgists insist) we should certainly kneel on Good Friday. Then if we are to place ourselves as offerings at his sacred feet, the order is "all that we are" and then "all that we have". The problem with this composition is that it neither feels like nor reads like a prayer that anyone would pray if present on Mount Calvary on Good Friday.

Conclusion

The Church of God, and the jurisdiction of it called the Church of England, is most certainly called by God to daily prayer, to unceasing prayer. To this end her members in the parishes of the land do need help, and for centuries that help in England has been primarily the fixed pattern and content of the Morning and Evening Prayer of the *Prayer Book*, which includes, importantly, the substantial readings from the Old and New Testaments, and the daily use of several psalms to make a monthly praying of the whole Psalter. To these basic services clergy and people have added as desired, or as possible, the ancient service of Compline (translated from the Latin) and sometimes a short service at noon. For none of these services has any special preparation has been needed apart from finding the appointed readings from the Bible and psalms set for the day. In the new world of *Common Worship* the times of prayer remain but the means of utilising them has changed, becoming more complicated and at times less obviously orthodox.

After working through the contents of *Common Worship: Daily Prayer* and comparing it with its literary parent, *Celebrating Common Prayer*, one is left with the very clear sense that the liturgists believe that the day of fixed texts for daily prayer is over and gone, and that

1 p. 318

the provision of such in *The Book of Common Prayer* is obsolete, except perhaps for Sunday and for those who will not enter into the new age of enlightened liturgy. The new way of prayer for Anglicans is apparently a way that revels in identifying a good shape or structure, searching for appropriate ingredients, and bringing all together to produce something which is relevant, satisfying or exciting for different times and places, occasions and types of users. The day of the large-scale *Directory* has arrived. If such an approach can ever be efficacious and successful in truly drawing people into the contemplation and adoration of the Holy and Righteous God and into the joyful service of Jesus Christ as Lord, then not only a tremendous amount of time but also great knowledge, skill and sensitivity are required to make it work. And, we must add, the use of many ribbons or alternatively much use of the laser printer.

Then also this complex task needs theological learning, for a duty is laid upon liturgists, whether national or local, to conform their productions to the teaching of sacred Scripture, the basic doctrine in the Anglican Formularies and the ecumenical dogma in the Three Creeds. The evidence of both *Celebrating Common Prayer* and *Daily Prayer* as well as *New Patterns for Worship* is that the liturgists are still in the learning curve in terms of the maturing of idea and expression. On too many occasions they have gone into print with rather poor ingredients. Further, to expect local worship leaders to have the necessary knowledge, wisdom and skill to create services that can truly merit the description of services of public worship is to expect far too much. In her desire to be relevant, open to all, intelligible and wide ranging in her provisions, the Church of England has flooded the market with too many goods and is unrealistically expecting inexperienced liturgical shoppers to choose wisely.

CHAPTER SIX

Baptism & Confirmation

Despite the fact that religion is for many people a privatised faith, there are still many families who do not attend church regularly but wish their infants to be "christened" or "baptized" in church. Not all these children, however, proceed after Baptism to Confirmation when they are sufficiently mature to appreciate the meaning and commitment of their baptism. Nevertheless, Confirmation services are still common in English parishes and provide occasion for the visit of the Bishop.

In *The Book of Common Prayer* there are two services for Holy Baptism, one for infants and one for adults—"The Order of Baptism both Publick and Private" and "The Order of Baptism for those of Riper Years"—and one "Order of Confirmation". *The Alternative Service Book 1980* has a collection of services under the general title of "Initiation Services", including services of thanksgiving for a child, of baptism, of confirmation, and combinations of these at both Holy Communion and Morning and Evening Prayer. We may note that the word "initiation", though used sparingly in the Early Church of Baptism, has entered liturgical language in modern times rather because of the general influence of anthropology and the "rites of initiation" much discussed by this science. *Common Worship* has in the main volume services of "Thanksgiving for the Gift of a Child" and "Holy Baptism" but there is also another whole volume entitled *Initiation Services*, wherein are the service outlines and possible ingredients for Baptism, Confirmation, and Reception into the Church of England. Further, the Liturgical Commission is planning to produce more services for this "journey" of what they see as "Christian Initiation".

Background

It has long been known by scholars that the administration of Baptism and Confirmation according to the *Prayer Book* is not modelled on that of the Early Church, when the majority of those baptized were adult converts, but on that of the later Western Church, when the vast majority of those baptized were infants. In this situation, what had earlier been done together, Baptism with Confirmation (laying on of hands) as one rite, was separated so that the baptized infant later had the opportunity of, in a sacramental kind of way, publicly appropriating the faith, grace and effects of his Baptism. Such a method has within it a sound psychology for it both receives children as infants and receives them again, after they have been instructed, as young persons who can now understand what it is they have embraced and Who it is that has embraced them.

It became somewhat unfashionable to defend the method of the *Prayer Book* during the period after World War II when much concern was expressed about indiscriminate infant baptism in parishes and when there was intense study and interest in the history of the practice and doctrine of Baptism, Chrismation and Confirmation. There were significant Reports to the General Synod on such topics in the 1970s which had their effect upon the services provided in *The Alternative Service Book 1980*. Further, Baptism became a major topic for ecumenical study at the highest level and the so-called Lima Document, *Baptism, Eucharist and Ministry* (1982), reveals some of the agreement and disagreement in the World Council of Churches. What seems to have gained much acceptance is the conviction that Christian initiation is complete in Baptism. This meant of course that for Anglicans and Lutherans Confirmation became a sacramental rite in search of a theology or even of justification. Then also the practice of Chrismation, the anointing with oil after the immersion in or pouring on of water, began to be widely adopted, especially since diocesan bishops have adopted the custom of blessing oils on Maundy Thursday in their cathedrals for the use of the parochial clergy. But this ceremony was without an agreed clear theology. In the light of all this debate and continuing discussion it is not surprising that the position adopted concerning what is now usually called "initiation" in *Common Worship* is not identical with that adopted in *The Alternative Service Book 1980*, and both are different from that of the *Prayer Book*. In fact, under the heading of "Approaching the Services" of *Common Worship* we are advised as follows:

> It is important to come to these services with a fresh mind, trying to put aside the approaches which have conditioned thinking while the *A[lternative] S[ervice] B[ook 1980]* has been in use. The authorized text needs to be seen not as an intrusive legal regulation but as a guide to performance".[1]

This may suggest not only that is it believed that the new services

1 *Initiation Services*, p. 8

have the right shape and content but also that the problem of what
to do with both Chrismation and Confirmation has been solved.
A new, exciting adventure apparently begins in Christian initiation,
and if one word can name it, that word is "journey" (or
"pilgrimage"). In fact this motif and paradigm is so powerful that it
tends to absorb all other themes and models used in Scripture and
tradition.

As already noted, the provision of services for "Christian
initiation" in *Common Worship* is found not only in the main volume[1]
but also in greater detail in *Common Worship: Initiation Services*,
actually published in 1998, two years before the main volume. All
these services are authorized pursuant to Canon B2 of the Canons of
the Church of England. This volume from 1998 contains "A
Commentary by the Liturgical Commission" on initiation.[2] There is
also an excellent chapter in the *Companion to Common Worship*
providing the background to and meaning of the services, indicating
where they differ from those of 1662 & 1980. From these sources and
elsewhere we learn that the shape and ingredients of the new services
of initiation were very much influenced by the recommendations of a
working party from two General Synod Boards (Education and
Mission) and the Liturgical Commission contained in a joint Report
entitled *Towards an Integrated Approach to Christian Initiation* (1995).
From this source the Liturgical Commission adopted a checklist of
the five elements of Christian Initiation, with each element having a
series of sub-headings. First of all there is the fact and context of the
church as the society of baptized people; secondly, the necessity of
warm welcome to enquirers; in the third place the need for prayer in
the church for the enquirers and converts; fourthly, the reality of "the
Way" of new disciples learning of Christ; fifthly, there is the goal of
true worship and service for all the baptized. The services already
published and those to be made available later are seen as coming
within these pastoral guidelines.

The theology in the new services is based on the Liturgical
Commission's belief that baptism involves four basic elements—
separation from the world (in those aspects where it is seen as
alienated from God); reception into a universal community centred
on God; growth within this community into the fullness of the
pattern of Christ; and sharing within this community in mission with
God's Spirit. In the explanation of these themes, the dominant image
is again that of *journey*—from the world into the church, within the
church through different stages of maturity and responsibility, and
then as the church in the world as a witnessing, pilgrim people,

1 pp. 337–75
2 pp. 185ff.

moving towards the goal, the Kingdom of Heaven. And, it is held, it is necessary to make liturgical provision for the whole of this journey, not only for its first decisive moment, Baptism, and what precedes and immediately follows it. Thus significant, later stages of the journey need to be marked by forms of service and these can include such things as reconciliation (confession, penance) in case of straying from the way; affirmation of baptismal faith in case of lapse or of new forms of commitment; of healing; of deliverance from addiction or bad habit or evil spirits; and of preparation for death, the end of the earthly part of the journey.

Since the Liturgical Commission seems to have taken on in its provision for initiation and pilgrimage a tremendously varied and in part controversial amount of theology, liturgy and pastoralia, we cannot begin here to evaluate all of it, even if it were all actually available. (What is available now is open to revision and what is not yet available could be provided over a period of several years and then revised.) Instead, we shall concentrate on the central shape and ingredients of the Baptism and Confirmation Services.

Baptism

The Lord Jesus Christ gave clear instructions to his disciples to make converts and to baptize them. At the end of the Gospel according to St Matthew we hear him say, "All power is given unto me in heaven and on earth. Go ye therefore and teach all nations, baptizing them in the name of the Father, and of the Son, and of the Holy Ghost, teaching them to observe all things whatsoever I have commanded you" (28: 18–19). At the end of the Gospel according to St Mark we hear the same Jesus say, "Go ye into all the world, and preach the Gospel to every creature. He that believeth and is baptized shall be saved; he that believeth not shall be damned" (16: 15–16). And near the beginning of the Gospel according to St John we hear Jesus say to Nicodemus, "Verily, verily I say unto thee, unless a man be born of water and of the Spirit, he cannot see the Kingdom of God" (3:3). In the Acts of the Apostles, St Luke records the words of the Apostle Peter before the first baptisms on the Day of Pentecost after the Ascension of Jesus: "Repent and be baptized every one of you, in the name of Jesus Christ for the remission of sins; and ye shall receive the gift of the Holy Ghost" (2: 38). Then in the Epistles, the apostles provide rich teaching on the purpose and meaning of baptism, using a variety of images.[1] So Baptism became the first Sacrament of the Church, the outward and visible gate of entry into the Household of God and the Body of Christ.

1 See e. g. Romans 6: 1–11; Titus 3:5; Galatians 3:27; and Hebrews 6:4 and 10:32.

Unlike the *Prayer Book* of 1662, which provides two services of Baptism (one for infants and a new one meant for missionary situations in the emerging British Empire), *Common Worship* provides one basic service (in terms of basic shape and required ingredients) to be used for all those to be baptized whether they be infants or old folks. We are told that

> For both infants and adults the service has the same inner logic, a movement from welcome and renunciation through to an identification with the people of God in their dependence upon God, their profession of the saving name, and the common activities of prayer, eucharist and mission. The different life circumstances of the newly baptized finds [*sic*] expression in the very different form that the Commission takes in each case.[1]

So the shape is as follows: Greeting, Liturgy of the Word and Liturgy of Baptism (Presentation of Candidates, Decision, Signing with the Cross, Prayer over the Water, Profession of Faith, Baptism, Commission, Prayers of Intercession, Welcome and Peace).

The signing with the cross is before the baptism and thus differs from the position in the *Prayer Book*, where immediately after the baptism the priest makes the sign of the cross on the forehead of the baptized and says,

> We receive this Child into the Congregation of Christ's flock and do sign him with the sign of the Cross, in token that hereafter he shall not be ashamed to confess the faith of Christ crucified and manfully to fight under his banner against sin, the world, and the devil, and to continue Christ's faithful soldier and servant unto his life's end.

In the new service, immediately after the Decision and before the Prayer over the Water, the minister makes the sign of the cross on the forehead of each candidate, and says, "Christ claims you for his own. Receive the sign of his cross." Then parents, godparents and sponsors are invited also to make the sign of the cross on the foreheads of the candidates, after which the minister says, "Do not be ashamed to confess the faith of Christ crucified" and the people then join in saying, "Fight valiantly as a disciple of Christ against sin, the world and the devil, and remain faithful to Christ to the end of your life." The justification for the place of the signing in the new services can be based upon the larger theme of journey:

> The pre-baptismal position for the signing fits well with the catechumenal approach to baptism and allows the Decision to be seen as the climax of a period of spiritual preparation, where the sign of the cross is a badge of Christian discipleship embraced after the decision and before the waters of death and resurrection.[2]

1 *Initiation Services*, p. 193   2 *Ibid.*, p. 197

Or it can be based upon the idea of ritual response:

> The signing with the cross comes as a ritual response to the decision made by the candidates. Since they have repented of their sins and committed themselves to the way of Christ, the Church marks them with his sign as a symbol of his acceptance of their decision, their belonging to him, and their new identity as disciples of the crucified one.[1]

These explanations having been noted, it is difficult to see compelling reasons why the signing could not have been left where it had been for over three centuries, where it has a simple logic of dramatic identification of a new child of God with Christ the crucified one. In fact the rubrics actually allow this to happen if the minister so determines.

The "Prayer over the Water" is the central prayer of the new rite and also contains "the main theological statement about baptism". So we must carefully examine it. Our confidence in it is not given a boost when we learn that its ancestry is not some patristic source but the American 1979 Prayer Book, via the Canadian 1985 *Book of Alternative Services*, together with some input from the latest New Zealand Prayer Book.[2] None of these sources is renowned for its classic orthodoxy!

It begins with the praise of God and the call for thanksgiving to him, including the response, if you are using *Initiation Services*, "It is right to give him thanks and praise,"[3] but if you are using the main volume of *Common Worship*, "It is right to give thanks and praise."[4] In the space of two years from the authorization of the first to that of the second, the demands of the feminist lobby had been heard and the masculine pronoun disappeared, as God apparently lost his masculine gender.

The Prayer itself has three paragraphs. The first gives thanks for the gift of water and its use in human life generally, and this leads on to a recital of mighty acts of God wherein water is prominent—the Holy Spirit moving over the waters (Genesis 1); the Exodus through water of the children of Israel; and the Baptism of Jesus in the river Jordan. In the second paragraph, there is thanksgiving for the water of baptism wherein "we are buried with Christ in his death" and by it "we share in his resurrection" and through it "we are reborn by the Holy Spirit". In the final paragraph there is petition for the sanctifying of the water in the font, that those who are baptized in it may be cleansed from sin, born again, renewed in the divine image, walk by the light of faith, and continue for ever in the risen life of Christ.

1 *Companion*, p. 166   2 *Ibid.*, p. 168
3 *Initiation Services*, p. 23   4 *Common Worship*, p. 355

Perhaps it needs to be observed that in the space of under 200 words this prayer incorporates a large variety of natural and biblical themes. To follow all this and understand it, when it is read out in a service, must require concentration and an above-average knowledge of the Bible, which few at a Baptismal Service would normally possess. Yet, as it were at the other extreme, the opening sentence unnecessarily simplifies. One wonders why it was necessary to add in the opening sentence after the "gift of water" the further words "to sustain, refresh and cleanse all life". Most people know what is the use of water and the American 1979 *Book of Common Prayer* simply has, "We thank you, Almighty God, for the gift of water." Then, if this Prayer over the Water is really a prayer, why does it take the form of telling God what he already knows and knows with perfection? He is told that "through water you led" and "in water your Son Jesus received" and "we are buried in the water of baptism". Further, it is as if he, the Master, were being commanded by his servants in the words, "Now sanctify this water ... ." In contrast in *The Book of Common Prayer*, the information which forms the basis of the petition for the sanctification of the water for the mystical washing away of sin, is presented, by means of relative clauses, as recollection before God of authentic parts of the total standing before and addressing of God and without presuming that he needs to be reminded of (in this case) the shedding of blood by the Son of God incarnate for our salvation. And the petition for sanctifying of the water begins in a suitably humble way, recognizing to whom we are speaking: "Regard, we beseech thee, the supplications of thy Congregation; Sanctify ... ."

But apart from the style of addressing the Almighty Father, the question must be asked whether too much emphasis is placed upon the *water* in "the water of baptism" as the means by which union with Jesus Christ unto salvation is brought into reality. The *Prayer Book* recognizes the sanctifying of water to the mystical washing away of sin, but the actual divine operation of spiritual washing, sanctifying and receiving of the candidate into the Body of Christ and Household of God is solely and only by and with the Holy Ghost. The second paragraph of the Prayer over the Water of the new rite reads:

> We thank you, Father, for the water of baptism.
> In it we are buried with Christ in his death.
> By it we share in his resurrection.
> Through it we are reborn by the Holy Spirit.

This language is probably too realistic and therefore in this day and age open to being interpreted literally. If we go back to the

Catechism of the *Prayer Book*, from which we take the basic lines of our sacramental doctrine, we learn that there are two parts to the Sacrament of Baptism, the outward visible sign and the inward spiritual grace. The outward part is water wherein the person is baptized/dipped, and the inward and spiritual part is "a death unto sin, and a new birth unto righteousness: for being by nature born in sin, and the children of wrath, we are hereby made the children of grace". The latter is effected by the Holy Ghost; the conveyance of grace and spiritual gifts has nothing to do with the water as such. God has ordained the use of water and this use is therefore necessary but it is also symbolic. The water even as set apart for this holy use contains no divine properties of healing of the soul.

In the new last paragraph we read:

> Now sanctify this water that, by the power of your Holy Spirit,
> they may be cleansed from sin and born again.

This can be taken to mean that after God sanctifies the water as requested, the power of the Holy Spirit will make it, the water, the means of the inner cleansing from sin and new birth. In other words, the sanctifying of the water, which is important for the Sacrament, is not sufficiently carefully distinguished from the inner sanctification of the human soul by the Holy Ghost. In the one case, the water is set apart for a holy and symbolic use; in the other case sanctification is a spiritual setting apart of the person from sin into the kingdom of God and his righteousness.

In Appendix 2 to the Holy Baptism of *Initiation Services*, under the title of "Seasonal Material", appear a further three Prayers over the Water, supplied for use at Epiphany, Easter/Pentecost and All Saints. Two of these Prayers happily do not attempt to tell the Almighty Lord what he knows already, though one does, that for All Saints. But when it comes to the content of the Prayers all three have petitions which move outside the doctrine of the Catechism. The Prayer for use at Epiphany requests:

> May your holy and life-giving Spirit
> move upon these waters.
> Restore through them the beauty of your creation,
> and bring those who are baptized
> to new birth in the family of your Church.

Here there seems to be a request for the water to effect the restoration of the created order to its pristine condition (which recalls the statement about worship and the promise God makes for all creation in the Preface of the main volume—see above, Chapter One). And the Prayer for use at All Saints requests:

Fill these waters, we pray, with the power of that same Spirit,
that all who enter them may be reborn,
and rise from the grave to new life in Christ.

Again, it seems as though it is the water as energized by the Spirit of
God that will effect the rebirth and resurrection.

Looking back to the Prayer over the Water in *The Alternative
Service Book 1980* we find a keener appreciation of the distinction
long held in Anglican doctrine. The priest prays (in prose):

Bless this water, that your servants who are washed in it may be
made one with Christ in his death and resurrection, to be
cleansed and delivered from all sin. Send your Holy Spirit upon
them to bring them to new birth in the family of your Church,
and raise them with Christ to full and eternal life.

While there is an element of realism in the first petition, the second
asking for the descent of the Holy Spirit is clear that it is he and no
other who causes internal cleansing and regeneration.

We noticed that the origins of the Prayer over the Water went back to
the American Prayer Book of 1979. It seems also that from this same
source comes the social and political dimension of the commitment
made by the newly baptized at the end of the service in the "Commission". One of the great phrases of the revolutionary 1960s was
"seeking peace and justice" and this entered the baptismal service in
the American Episcopal Church. Because it was regarded as part of
the "Baptismal Covenant" made freely with God by the baptized, it
became the basis for many calls and not a few programmes of social,
economic and political kinds generated by the General Convention
of the Episcopal Church. Peace and justice can take a strict biblical
meaning or they can so easily take an activist political secular
meaning suited to modern peace and liberation movements. In the
Episcopal Church all kinds of human rights movements have used
these words as the basis of their right to acceptance in church and
society, especially, in recent times, the lesbigays. In the new English
service, imitating the older American service, the newly baptized are
asked: "Will you acknowledge Christ's authority over human society,
by prayer for the world and its leaders, by defending the weak, and
by seeking peace and justice?" To which they answer, "With the help
of God, I will." It is highly probable that much the same use will be
made of the theme of "seeking of peace and justice" by groups within
the Church of England as has already been made by powerful lobbies
in the Episcopal Church of the USA.

Another theological trend common in the Episcopal Church and
intimately related to baptism and the baptismal covenant is the claim
that since initiation is complete in baptism, then all gifts of ministry

are also given in potentiality in baptism and lie in the soul awaiting to become active. It is the sacrament that has within it the seeds of all possible and future forms of ministry. Such a doctrine allows a person when ordained to say, "This is a realisation of what was there in embryo in my baptism." When the present Presiding Bishop, Frank Griswold, was installed in the National Cathedral in Washington, he boldly stated that this was an outworking of the meaning of his baptism. But it also serves the radical cause very well for it allows persons of both sexes, the few who are bisexual, and those of gay or lesbian sexual orientation, to claim a right to ordination as they are, because in their baptisms, as they were, they were given in potentiality the gift of all the church's ministries. He or she who is baptized, whatever his or her sexual orientation, is potentially a deacon, a priest, a bishop and a primate. How far this type of thinking will be used to press radical agendas in the Church of England time will tell.

Confirmation

What is the biblical basis of Confirmation? It has long been argued that in the time of the apostles and evangelists the normal procedure for admitting converts to Christianity into the membership of the Catholic Church, the Household of God, was by baptism (usually immersion in water) and with the laying on of hands.[1] If this is so, then why has Confirmation as such been treated as separate from Baptism for so long in the history of the Church in the West? It is well known that Confirmation has been regarded by many in the Latin, Western Church as one of the Seven Sacraments and though related to Baptism, yet distinct from it and having a biblical foundation in the apostolic laying on of hands upon converts to Jesus Christ. However, in terms of historical development, the rite of Confirmation is what was once the concluding part of the rich service administered by the local church in the late patristic era of the Baptism of households, adults and children. The reason for this division of the patristic baptismal rite into two was that the vast majority of those being baptized in the early Middle Ages were infants of already baptized parents. The provision of another rite or sacrament made it possible for infants, baptized when they were not fully conscious of what was happening to them, to be blessed later in life by the Bishop and to be publicly incorporated into the Church and their Christian duties. At the Reformation in the sixteenth century, the reformed Church of England retained the Rite of Confirmation as distinct from Baptism, primarily for use with

---

1 Acts 8:14–17 and 19:1–7; Hebrews 6:2; 2 Corinthians 1:22; Ephesians 1:13 & 4:30

children who having been baptized as infants were now old enough to speak for themselves.

According to the *Prayer Book* the infant children of baptized parents should themselves be baptized as soon as possible after birth and then be brought to Confirmation when older, usually seven years of age and above, when they have been taught the Catechism. Adult converts to Christianity are to be baptized and then confirmed as soon as possible afterwards. Thus Baptism is seen as a Sacrament which is complete in terms of salvation and as a means of entry into the kingdom of God and into the Body of Christ, the Church of God. Yet there is a sense in which Baptism is incomplete, the sense of perfecting a baptized person's relation to Christ and his Church. The relation is to be brought to fulfilment by Confirmation so that each child of God can walk rightly in the strength of the Holy Ghost. The infant growing into the young person needs to make his very own the vows made for him by godparents and also to receive the strengthening of the Holy Ghost, by the laying on of hands and prayer of the Bishop. The older person also needs the laying on of hands to receive the gifts of the Holy Ghost, in order to live the Christian life in the fullness of the Spirit within the Body of Christ. In this approach, one's first reception of Holy Communion is normally but not necessarily after Confirmation.

Whether it is held at the Eucharist or with Morning or Evening Prayer, the shape and content of the new service of Confirmation in *Common Worship* is the same. Its ingredients are the Greeting, the Liturgy of the Word and the Liturgy of Initiation (Presentation, Decision, Profession of Faith, Confirmation, Commission and Peace). Within this Liturgy of Initiation, Confirmation itself is quite short, beginning with the traditional versicles and responses (Psalms 124:8 & 113:2). The Bishop, who alone takes this service, then extends his hands towards those to be confirmed and asks God to cause his Spirit to rest upon these baptized persons. He continues by laying his hand on the head of each one, saying, "Confirm, O Lord, your servant with your Holy Spirit." Finally, the whole congregation prays for those confirmed using words suggested by the Bishop's own prayer in the *Prayer Book*, "Defend, O Lord, your servants ... ."

Confirmation continues to be a popular service in parishes in the life of the Church of England even though there has been very little if any positive publicity given to it within the Church in recent times. The Liturgical Commission comments:

> The high pastoral profile of confirmation within the mission of the Church was largely a development of the nineteenth century and there is continuing debate about its precise relation to admission to communion and to the development of mature faith

in those baptized in infancy. ... The confirmation services authorized in this provision follow carefully traditional Anglican practice and make no attempt to resolve these difficult questions. On all views confirmation derives its meaning from baptism. The structure of the confirmation services therefore conforms to the baptism service and has a similar inherent logic and flow.[1]

This means that there are definite similarities between the whole service in the *Prayer Book* and the part of the Liturgy of Initiation called "Confirmation" in the modern service, but the similarity is via the Canadian *Book of Alternative Services*, upon whose service of Confirmation that in *Common Worship* is specifically based.

Isaiah 11:2 ("And the Spirit of the Lord shall rest upon him, the Spirit of wisdom and understanding ... ") is the key biblical text for the historical meaning of Confirmation as a distinctive rite. It is the basis of the reference in the Western tradition to the seven-fold gift of the Holy Ghost given to the Messiah, and from him to his people. This reference to the seven-fold gift, which is very clear in the *Prayer Book*, is maintained, though less clearly, in this new service. This is because its use of Isaiah 11:3 is a straight borrowing from *The Alternative Service Book 1980* and not a modern rendering of the words in the *Prayer Book*. The Prayer in the 1662 Service makes it clear that it is the traditional seven-fold gift of grace that is being sought from God, while the new prayer from 1980 can be taken as referring only to a six-fold gift, because it does not say, "the spirit of thy holy fear" but "let their delight be in the fear of the Lord."

The laying on of a hand by the bishop on each candidate is also maintained in the new service but again not with the same words as in 1662 but rather using those from 1980. Thus the Bishop does not say as he lays his hand upon the head of every candidate, "Defend, O Lord, this thy child/servant with thy heavenly grace ... " as in the *Prayer Book*, but, says, rather, as in the 1980 service, "Confirm, O Lord, your servant with your Holy Spirit." However, the well-known prayer, "Defend, O Lord ... ", is retained, following the 1980 service, but as a congregational prayer for the newly confirmed.

Because the Liturgical Commission apparently holds that Confirmation is really a "pastoral rite" (as it is called in the American 1979 Prayer Book) and is a ceremony in search of a theology, it has deliberately not supplied it with the context and doctrine that it contains in *The Book of Common Prayer* (1662). Here the opening Preface makes clear who should be confirmed and for what purpose. Those who were baptized as infants and have learned the Catechism should come before the Bishop so that they can with their own mouths and consent ratify and confirm before him and the

---

1 *Initiation Services*, p. 202

church the promises made for them by their godparents and go forth to live as faithful Christians. The Bishop in turn prays for them that they will be strengthened by the presence of the Holy Ghost and by the imparting to them the seven-fold gifts of the Spirit of Messiah. Then he lays his hand on each of them and asks God to defend, protect and keep them by his grace as his faithful children for ever. Further, after the Lord's Prayer, comes the Collect in which the Bishop again prays for those confirmed: "Let thy fatherly hand, we beseech thee, ever be over them; let thy Holy Spirit ever be with them; and so lead them in the knowledge and obedience of thy Word, that in the end they may obtain everlasting life … ."

While theologians and liturgists debate the finer points of initiation and constantly seek to show that Confirmation was not in the Early Church a sacrament in its own right, and while ecumenical agreements with Lutheran and Methodists seem to make Confirmation by the Bishop out of place and unnecessary, there can be no doubt but that, at the parish level, the *Prayer Book* service of Confirmation is still popular and does work today in most social settings when there is a will to make it do so. It provides not only a goal which young people in the church can be inspired to desire and move towards, but it also provides a sound reason for them to be instructed in the basics of the faith, the Creed, the Commandments, the Lord's Prayer and the Beatitudes, as starters. Further, its verbal content is memorable and moving and leaves a profound impression upon young minds. And it is compact enough to fit easily into either Morning or Evening Prayer or Holy Communion from the same *Prayer Book.*

It is worthy of note that the first Confirmation service conducted by Dr Rowan Williams as Archbishop of Canterbury, in his Cathedral, was of sixty young people and using the *Prayer Book* service.

Summary

Certainly for those who are fascinated by study of ancient baptismal liturgies and catechetical schools, and who also find pleasure in trying out new shapes and ingredients for modern services of baptism, what is going on in the Church of England now under the heading of Initiation is exciting and stimulating. The ferment, which began before the appearance of the provisions for initiation in 1980, continues to this day, fuelled by more study, the creation of more services, and the implications of inter-communion agreements between churches. At the same time, an ordinary person who begins to try to read and understand *Common Worship: Initiation Services* will probably find himself utterly confused and wonder why there is so much choice and so many options. We are reasonably attuned to choice in everything from life-style to consumer goods as people living in the western world, but the variety of this volume is so overwhelming as to make even such persons wonder what virtue there can be in multiple choice for such a basic thing in Christianity as Holy Baptism. After all, what is really important are the words, "I baptize thee in the Name of the Father and the Son and the Holy Ghost". And when so much is produced to surround these words the principle of "quality control" is in danger of being compromised or forgotten. What we have ended up with is a lot of mediocre liturgy wherein are doctrinal statements open to serious misunderstanding, clothed in a rather flat and dull English, which ends up being hardly worthy of the high vocation to which it is put—of the entry of the sinner into the family of God for communion with the Holy Trinity and the gift of eternal life.

CHAPTER SEVEN

Pastoral Services

Some people may perhaps be surprised, when they open the volume entitled *Common Worship: Pastoral Services*, to find that the Introduction is devoted to the theme of "The Journey". We are told that

> We are all on a journey through life. One of the presuppositions on which the Church of England's Pastoral Services are based is that we do not travel alone. Where is God in relation to that journey? He is both the starting point and the ending point, the Alpha and the Omega. Not only that but ... in all our rushing around between the beginning and the end, he is there too.[1]

Yet, on reflection and recalling the intriguing reference in the Preface of the main volume of *Common Worship* to worship and liturgy as a kind of journey or pilgrimage, and then the prominent use of the image of journey in *Common Worship: Initiation Services*, we are not surprised that journeying should again be the predominant image for the context and meaning of such services as marriage and the burial of the dead—though, it seems, a badly organized journeying ("rushing around") which does not seem likely to get anywhere.

Within *Pastoral Services* there are provisions and resources for Wholeness and Healing, Marriage, Emergency Baptism, Thanksgiving for a Child, and Ministry before, at and after Funerals. Again we learn that

> Through all of these resources runs the theme of being accompanied on the journey by the Church, by the people who, in surrounding and supporting us, reveal the personal love and care of Jesus Christ, whose death put an end to death for eternity.
>
> The pastoral task of the Christian Church, all the people of God, ministers and laity, is to provide company on the journey, towards baptism, marriage, welcoming children and at death itself.[2]

1 *Common Worship: Pastoral Services*, p. 3   2 *Ibid.*, p. 6

Those who adopt the metaphor of the journey so predominantly and thoroughly run the risk of seeing everything in the light of it and thus interpreting the Christian life and vocation in a restricted way. Certainly the vocation of the pilgrim, the walking in the Way of Christ, the walking in the Spirit, and the pressing on to the goal of the high calling of God in Christ Jesus, are strong biblical themes, and they are to be embraced by the Household of God, which is the Body of Christ. But there are other images and metaphors such as the Christian life as a constant battle with enemies (those invisible and visible powers which seek to do harm to the church of God, each individual believer and the cause of Christ—see Ephesians 6). We are told to become as little children, and as such in his Epistles St John habitually addresses us. The Bible frequently calls us members of a body, a household, a family, and even more frequently a flock of sheep. All these images are much used in hymns, but in *Common Worship* they have given place altogether to this *journey*.

The danger in the West, where people have become used to the comfortable life with a pill for every pain and discomfort, is that *the journey* will be understood creatively, colourfully and imaginatively and yet as pointing to something easy, pain-free and without difficult mountains to climb, dangerous rapids to cross, wild animals to avoid or kill, and stinking swamps to negotiate. These last are not mentioned in the brochures of the most popular contemporary journeys, the package tours. The walking with the Lord Jesus in the Spirit towards the Father's glory is the highest of privileges and vocations, but it is a hard and tough way with privation, tribulation and persecution. "Believe not those who say / The upward path is smooth." In the Sermon on the Mount the Lord Jesus urged us: "Enter ye in at the strait gate, for wide is the gate and broad is the way that leadeth to destruction, and many there be who go in thereat; because strait is the gate, and narrow is the way which leadeth unto life, and few there be that find it" (Matthew 7:13–14). The Way of the Father in which Jesus himself walked was the very opposite of easy and smooth, for it was exceedingly narrow all the way and headed straight for Mount Calvary *via* the Judean desert and the Garden of Gethsemane. Therefore, he said to his disciples: "Take up your cross and follow me." Is that the journey to which *Common Worship* invites us?

Healing Services

In the "Theological Introduction"[1]—produced by a theologian rather than a liturgist?—to the services and resources on "Wholeness

1 *Common Worship: Pastoral Services*, pp. 9–11

and Healing" there is strangely no mention of journeying! However, evil forces are recognized to be at work in the world:

> This series of pictures [of evil powers], while not absolving us from personal responsibility for our actions, also strongly implies that without the grace of God we are at risk of being in the grip of an array of forces beyond our powers to resist or break.

Here the full reality of Satan and evil forces in the world is somewhat understated and minimised. These spiritual antagonistic realities surround and embrace us much more than we commonly know or admit. They ambush us constantly as we walk in the way of Christ and thus we need, in Paul's words, to be protected by the Christian armour and stay alongside our fellow soldiers in the army of Christ Jesus, the Captain of our salvation. The apostle's description of the "whole armour of God" in Ephesians 6 is as relevant today as it was in A.D. 60.

Certainly in the Church of God no-one should walk towards Zion alone and no-one should fight evil alone for we are members one of another in the Body of Christ. We all know that it is much easier to speak of these things or to put together liturgies with introductions which emphasise togetherness, community, fellowship and being with and for each other, than it is to live this out practically day by day. We are fallen, sinful, human beings in the process of being sanctified. Such biblical and theological realism is to be read and felt in the Services of the *Prayer Book* for Marriage, the Visitation and Communion of the Sick and the Burial of the Dead. It is also found in these *Pastoral Services*, but in a somewhat diluted form, for occasionally the famous British heresy of Pelagianism (that the human will is basically good) makes its presence known.

It is regrettable that what is found here and there in *Pastoral Services* but not anywhere in the *Prayer Book* itself are hints of a vague universalism; that is, in the sense of this present world and all its creatures being ultimately regenerated and renewed by God. For example healing (explained as experiencing the work of the Holy Spirit) is said to be "a way of partaking in God's new life that will not be complete until it includes the whole creation and the destruction of death itself".[1] Here there seems to be no place for the wrath and judgement of God against sin and evil. In Prayer E we are directed to pray:

> Lord of all life,
> help us to work together for that day
> when your kingdom comes
> and justice and mercy will be seen in all the earth.[2]

This suggests the arrival of the kingdom without judgement and by human work. In a text provided to be read during a service of healing

1 p. 11   2 p. 58

we are told: "Jesus sets before us the hope of the kingdom of God. All that is broken will be bound up in God's healing love. All that is marred by weakness and sin will be transformed by God's reconciling love."[1] Will nothing be purified by the fires of the wrath of God against sin? Will not the kingdom of God be a wholly different sphere, reality and space to this present world and cosmos? What is the purpose of Christ's Second Coming to judge the living and the dead?

Another matter that has specific pastoral consequences and implications is the way in which absolutions and declarations of healing are presented in this volume, that is the way they are worded. Specifically, under what conditions should the word "May" be used? (We raised this matter briefly in Chapter Five when examining the Absolutions provided for use in Daily Prayer.) In *Pastoral Services* one sometimes gets the impression that the bishop and priest should pronounce an Absolution that is direct and that does not use "may". For example, when hands are laid upon a dying person only the priest (or bishop) is allowed to say:

> By the ministry of reconciliation,
> entrusted by Christ to his Church,
> receive his pardon and peace
> to stand before him in his strength alone,
> this day and evermore.

The deacon or lay person must say:

> May almighty God have mercy on you,
> forgive you your sins,
> and bring you to everlasting life.[2]

This seems to be the old distinction made in the Church of England that only those ordained priest can pronounce an absolution. However, this principle is not put into consistent practice: the rubrics state that the priest may use the second form if he wishes. Apparently in all the provisions for the laying on of hands and anointing with oil[3] the accepted form, whether spoken by priest or lay minister, is that which begins with "May". For example:

> May Christ bring you wholeness
> of body, mind and spirit,
> deliver you from every evil,
> and give you his peace.

The "May" form is also used for most blessings.[4] However, in the "Prayers for Protection and Peace",[5] presumably to be said by any kind of minister, the more direct form of addressing a person seeking divine blessing has found its way into the provisions:

1 p. 42   2 p. 221   3 pp. 92–3   4 E.g. p. 97   5 p. 95

Our Lord Jesus Christ,
present with us in his risen power,
enter into your body and spirit,
take from you all that harms and hinders you
and fill you with his healing and his peace.

Here a linguistic deed is being done, but in the "May" form of the others the whole business becomes tentative. Possibly for healing services such is the appropriate form! But if so this means that the whole thing is set in the context of possibility rather than a certainty that in some way, in part or in whole, the gift of healing is given.

The Marriage Service

In the Introduction to the whole *Pastoral Services* volume, the Marriage Service is said to be not for everyone as is Baptism. True enough, for the call to celibacy for the sake of the kingdom of God is still on the table! Nevertheless it is claimed for marriage that "here again the Church is present on the journey, surrounding the couple with love, providing preparation and promising—for the first time in a Church of England service—support and prayer."[1] The service itself is provided with a "Pastoral Introduction" to be read by those present as they sit and wait for the ceremony to begin. It may safely be assumed that its content tells us something important about how the liturgists and General Synod view marriage in general and this service in particular. If so, we are left wondering whether they are so affected by the modern divorce culture and sexual liaisons that they either have no really high doctrine of Christian marriage or, if they have one, no right words to describe it.

Before commenting on the actual doctrinal content of the Introduction, it is necessary to observe that it is a most disappointing literary piece. It is after all intended to be read silently not aloud and it needs to captivate the interest of people in the pews as they await the arrival of the bride. But it begins with the rather obvious information that "a wedding is one of life's great moments"! Then in its doctrinal statement of what God intends for marriage we are told, very much in the secular language of our time, that marriage is a "creative relationship". If there is one over-used word in modern English it is "relationship" and it usually points to a coming together freely of persons or groups for a short time and for a limited purpose. A relationship as such may be broken at will by either party. Further, it is an expression much used since the 1960s for making

---

1 *Pastoral Services*, p. 4. Stephen Lake in the practical guide *Using Common Worship: Marriage* (2000) praises "the innovative aspect" of presenting marriage as a "series of stages" on "a journey".

"acceptable" adulterous and illicit sexual unions. Christian marriage, in fact any genuine marriage, is much more than, and should be qualitatively much different from, a "relationship". The use of the term here merely confirms for people the low view of marriage in modern society and the right of either "partner" to end it at will.

In the Service itself a Statement of the nature and purpose of marriage is read out by the Minister and for this he or she has a choice between two discourses.[1] Each of them says touching things about marriage as a union of persons and as the foundation of family life. But neither of them has the realism of the Statement in the 1928 *Prayer Book* that marriage "was ordained [of God] in order that the natural instincts and affections, implanted by God, should be hallowed and directed aright; that those who are called of God to this holy estate, should continue therein in pureness of living." And, further, neither of them has the more definite realism of the older 1662 *Prayer Book* which states: "It was ordained for a remedy against sin, and to avoid fornication." The context of church marriage today is a society and culture which is drenched with illicit and abnormal sexual propaganda and activity, more so than in 1662 or 1928. But we today think it not nice to mention such obvious and realistic things "at one of life's great moments" and in connection with a God, who approves of niceness—a God who may be addressed at the beginning of the service in these terms: "God of wonder and of joy: grace comes from you, and you are the source of life and love." Turning to the vows made by each, it is to be noted that (if you turn to page 150 from page 108 or have provided for this option in your own local pamphlet) the woman may, if she so chooses, add "obey" to "love and cherish". To their credit, those who created this service still allowed for the possibility that some pious woman, having taken the words of the apostle Paul to heart that a wife is to submit to her husband as unto the Lord (Ephesians 5:22), decides she wants publicly to say "obey" in her vow at her marriage.

In the words that accompany the placing of the ring on the hand, the required ending is "within the love of God, Father, Son and Holy Spirit." This replaces "In the Name of the Father and of the Son and of the Holy Ghost" in the 1662 and 1928 *Prayer Book*s. It is difficult to conceive what "in the love of God, Father, Son and Holy Spirit" really means in this context, although the mention of love may be seen by some as giving the whole thing a "nice flavour". As created, finite beings we are not within the ineffable, holy Love that is God, the Love which unites the Three Persons in the one Godhead. A man and woman do not share all that they have within the love of God but they share as they each separately and both together seek to love

1 *Pastoral Services*, p. 105 and p. 136

God as he has commanded them to do, and as he sends the Holy Spirit to bring holy love to their souls. Better surely to make their promises in the Name of the Persons of the Holy Trinity even as long tradition recommends! The alternative Prayer[1] at the giving of the ring(s) also does not distinguish sufficiently clearly between the unique, eternal Love which is the eternal Essence of the relations between the Three Persons and the love that God gives to human beings according to their creaturely reality. What we receive as human beings is truly the love of God, his gift to us, but that love in a form receivable by finite creatures made in his image and after his likeness. The Prayer speaks of the heavenly Father, "source of everlasting love" which is "poured into our hearts". Then that love is described in terms recalling the Song of Solomon 8:6–7 as "that love which many waters cannot quench, neither floods drown". Finally, it speaks of the marriage covenant between the man and woman as made "in the love of your Son". It is not clear whether this is "in the loving of your Son" or "in the love of the Father which he reveals and bestows" or something else. Finally, on this theme of love and the distinction between God as Love and God as loving us we may note one of the optional blessings of the marriage:

> Eternal God,
> you create us out of love
> that we should love you and one another.
> Bless this man and this woman, made in your image,
> who today become a sign of your faithful love to us
> in Christ Jesus our Lord.[2]

This as read aloud sounds like the kind of prayer a modern clergyman or Reader would compose if he were asked to pray on the spot in an *ex tempore* way. Apart from the attempt to inform the Eternal One of what he decided in eternity, the prayer expresses the questionable doctrine that a couple by the act of marriage itself (which is their act done before God and man) actually become thereby "a sign of your faithful love to us in Christ Jesus our Lord".

In the "Additional Prayers"[3] frequent mention, as one would expect, is made of love; but, again, those who composed these prayers and vetted them did not have clear guidelines in their minds as to the nature and character of love as of God as God is in himself, as of human beings in the relations one with another, and as the merciful, compassionate attitude of God towards man in, through and with Jesus Christ and by the Holy Ghost. The petition, "May their life together be a sign of your love to this broken world" is acceptable if they are living as individuals and together according to

---

1 p. 151   2 p. 153   3 pp. 156ff.

God's laws and in the power of his Spirit as servants of Jesus Christ. However, the request that "as their love ripens and their marriage matures, they may reap the harvest of the Spirit, rejoice in your gifts, and reflect your glory" seems to make everything depend on their life together as a couple and to discount that fact that each of them always remains an individual person, with a body and soul, a mind, emotions and will, who is loved by God, needs to be individually purified and sanctified and to mature in faith, hope and love. The man and woman are united as one flesh not as one body and soul—a fact that not a few of the prayers seem not to have grasped, for they have "you have made one" not as "one flesh" (which truth is recognized in Prayer 2 on page 157). Finally, it is perhaps to be expected in the twenty-first century that the new prayer book of the Church of England would enlarge the New Testament vocabulary and meaning of love and include *eros* along with *philia* and *agape*. Thus one prayer begins, "God our creator, we thank you for the gift of sexual love [*eros*] by which husband and wife may delight in each other". It is not necessary to make what is so often mentioned in the world into a public prayer at a wedding.

It would seem that instead of providing a minimum of options and making every effort to guarantee the doctrine and quality of the prayers, the Liturgical Commission has given us so many options that the impression one gets of their overall quality is not a good one. The composition of suitable prayers for any occasion in public worship is difficult, and here it was made the more difficult because so many were provided it seems that they could not be carefully scrutinized.

The Funeral Service

The Funeral Service does not come alone (as in the *Prayer Book*) but together with the provision of services or outlines of services for use before the Funeral and after the Funeral, together with other sources—prayers, Bible readings, psalms and canticles, and even a theological essay. If Marriage is only loosely connected with the overall theme of "journey" the Funeral Service is tightly connected. "The Funeral Service," we are told,

> is both the end of the human journey in this world and a whole series of journeys in itself. ... As grieving is a process marked by different stages, we believe that one helpful contribution the Church can make pastorally is to have a series of services and resources in which some of these different stages can be recognized, spoken of in advance or recapitulated.

So "the Funeral Service is part of a longer continuum, though it stands perfectly well on its own if necessary." And "the bereaved will need to be able to say different things to God and to one another at each of these different stages."[1]

Usually modern liturgists do not want to copy or retain anything that developed in the Middle Ages for their eyes are upon the pristine, primitive Church. However, in this case, they have decided to create a modern equivalent for the Funeral rite and customs of the pre-Reformation period.

> From the eighth century or earlier, the Funeral rite was a continuum, broken by movements from place to place, from home to church, to the place of burial and back to the home. This pattern was severely truncated at the Reformation, but today's pastoral needs suggest a return to it.[2]

In other words, modern psychological and pastoral insights show the wisdom of the medieval practice and lie behind the provision of prayers and services for this continuum. What perhaps needs to be said here is that many clergy, using the various parson's or priest's handbooks that have long been available for guidance, have been doing as pastoral routines rather than liturgical tasks the kind of things here made into semi-official services and provisions. So the question arises as to whether a National Church needs anything more than a basic Funeral Service, with suitable provisions for infants, children and adults, in its Prayer Book. When so much is provided it is difficult to see the wood for the trees. Too many of the prayers, like those provided for marriage, are similar to good *ex tempore* prayers and, further, most of them attempt to tell God who he is, what is his character, what he has revealed, what he plans to do and will do and so on.

Turning to The Funeral Service,[3] we find that, like the marriage service, it has a Pastoral Introduction, to be read by those present before the service begins. Once more it has to be said that this is extremely disappointing as a literary production. Here was an opportunity to use a good "popular writer" to communicate the biblically-based Christian hope in words that are dignified and informative. Let us note the first of the two paragraphs:

> God's love and power extend over all creation. Every life, including our own, is precious to God. Christians have always believed that there is hope in death as in life, and that there is new life in Christ over death.

The first sentence is true enough as far as it goes but hardly the place or the way to start in a brief message to mourners. The second sentence is awkward in its construction and would have been better kept wholly personal, relating specifically to the one individual reading it. The

---

1 *Pastoral Services*, p. 5   2 *Ibid.*   3 pp. 256ff.

third and longest sentence expresses the Christian hope in a less than satisfactory way. The truth is not "that there is hope in death as in life". How can a dead person hope? The Christian virtue and gift of hope focuses rather upon God the Father and on what he has promised, in and through Jesus Christ, and will provide for his sake for baptized believers—eternal life in a resurrected, immortal, glorious body with all the redeemed in heaven. Thus the Christian hope is to be proclaimed at the Funeral Service, and is done so very clearly in that of the *Prayer Book* and in this service being considered here. Why not so also in the Pastoral Introduction? Further, what does "new life in Christ OVER death" mean? It is an odd expression.

Apart from any inadequacy of style, some of the optional prayers fail to rise to the level of biblical truth. At the beginning of the service God is told how he will judge the world: "Almighty God, you judge us with infinite mercy and justice and love everything you have made."[1] It may be asked: How can God the wholly righteous Lord judge the angels and man except by his justice? If in his infinite mercy he has provided One to stand in our place, even the Lord Jesus Christ, he still judges righteously and justly. His mercy provides what his justice requires, even the one Mediator, who died in our place and rose for our justification before God the Father.

Then in the confession of sins we are instructed to say: "We turn from the wrong that we have thought and said and done, and are mindful of all that we have failed to do." Do we really hold in mind at this moment of speech all, truly all, that we have failed to do, all our sins of omission?

In the Resources for the funeral of a child,[2] there is much that is touching and moving. However, one cannot but notice again the mediocre or poor quality of many of the thirty or so prayers provided for optional use. Better to have provided fewer of excellent quality. Prayer 9, for example, begins, "God of all mystery" and ends "we make our prayer in Jesus' name." In prayer in times of loss, the bereaved need to know that they pray to a Divine Person, the Almighty, heavenly Father. It is difficult to conceive of communion with and consolation from the "God of all mystery". Then the ending of the prayer is the kind so familiar in popular prayer meetings where *ex tempore* prayer is the norm, and does not sound or feel right in public prayer where a proper reverential and theological way of ending prayers has long been known and in use.

Again in the *ninety* or so "Prayers for use with the Dying and at Funeral and Memorial Services"[3] there is much that is touching and moving. Yet once more the quality of many of the prayers, as public prayers, is disappointing. Prayer 16 as a "Thanksgiving for the Life of

1 p. 260   2 pp. 300ff.   3 pp. 345ff.

the Departed" begins with the lofty words of St Paul in Ephesians 1,
"Blessed be the God and Father of our Lord Jesus Christ who has
blessed us." This surely leads us to expect a prayer filled with the
thought of divine grace given to the one being remembered. But the
prayer leaves the heavenly realms where Paul's thoughts were, in
order to descend immediately to earth and speak of "the gift of this
earthly life", "span of years and gift of character" and of "every good
deed done by him/her". In offering thanksgiving for the departed,
there is a fine line to tread between referring, on the one hand, to
their life so that God is praised and, on the other hand, suggesting
that their good works somehow in a little way actually help to earn
eternal salvation. Thus it is wise to compose prayers where no hint of
this latter idea appears. In Prayer 37 God is told that "you do not
willingly grieve or afflict your children." Maybe a "nice God" of our
imagination does not, but the God of the Bible, who loves us with an
everlasting love, does sometimes afflict us in order to test us, to
chastise us and to make us worthy to be called his adopted children.
And did not the Father afflict his Incarnate Son with the pain of
Gethsemane and Calvary for our sake and the world's salvation?

In contrast to the frequent mediocrity within general orthodoxy,
Prayer 57 shows signs of careful composition in order to present an
alternative view of God. It begins:

> Intimate God,
> you are able to accept in us
> what we cannot even acknowledge;

and continues by telling him (or is it her?) further matters before
making the request,

> Reconcile us through your cross
> to all that we have rejected in ourselves,
> that we may find no part of your creation
> to be alien or strange to us,

and ends "through Jesus Christ, our lover and our friend". The
identity of the intimate God, his/her relation to "your cross" and to
Jesus "our lover" are far from clear, nor is it clear why the Cross is
expected to reconcile us to the evil that we may have rejected in
ourselves.

The "Theological Note on the Funeral of a Child dying near the
time of Birth"[1] is hardly appropriate for a prayer book, however
erudite and thoughtful it is judged to be. The content of this Note is
said to draw upon advice given by Professor Oliver O'Donovan of
Christ Church, Oxford, but it is not clear what are the views of the

---

1 pp. 316–17

Professor and what are those of the Liturgical Commission. The reason for the Note is to make a contribution to the growing recognition of the need for particular care for those parents and families who have experienced the tragedy of an infant who dies near but before the time of birth. It is fully accepted that a funeral service is appropriate, but we are told that the words in the Committal, "in sure and certain hope of the resurrection to eternal life", raise two questions. The first is, "Is it right to regard an unborn child as a human person with a capacity for life after death?" And the second is, "Is it right to speak of 'a sure and certain hope' in the case of someone who has not lived outside the womb and has not been baptized?" What is said in answer to the second question tends to leave us with more questions than before it was raised. It states, for example, that "we are right to be cautious about a *particular* assertion of the individual child's resurrection" and that the text of the Committal provided for the service actually stops short of this assertion. However, seemingly in contradiction of this, the ending of Prayer 5 entitled "Stillbirth" on page 313 is: "We had longed to welcome him/her amongst us; grant us the assurance that he/she is now encircled in your arms of love, and shares the resurrection life of your Son, Jesus Christ." Also the next prayer, number 6, entitled "Miscarriage" (where the infant/foetus in question is probably less than 24 weeks) ends: "Grant them [parents] the assurance that their child, though not seen by us, is seen and known by you, and will share the risen life of your Son, Jesus Christ." It would have been far better not to have included this short essay and to have assumed that priests in their training in college and in parish would be directed both to read appropriate essays and also to learn from experienced pastors how to handle such situations.

Conclusion

Those who put *Pastoral Services* together certainly made a great effort to provide comprehensively for the parishes of England, and they have displayed all kinds of pastoral sensitivity. Nevertheless, however important and useful the pastoral sensitivities revealed in the texts of *Pastoral Services* may be, the fact of too much choice from that which is not often of the best quality reduces the value of this volume. At the local level, what the clergyman or local worship committee is faced with in this book as he/they plan a service of healing, a wedding service or minister to the dying and bereaved, is too much material—unless, that is, they have plenty of time on their hands. Certainly those who are experienced pastors will be able to put together biblically based and orthodox services from the plentiful provision, even if their idiom and style turns out to be somewhat ordinary and flat. And since the dominating theme of journey is not built into quite all the texts, it is possible to create services which allow full scope for other biblical and theological images of the vocation of a Christian on earth.

The marriage service is an occasion where the liturgy should realistically assess the human condition, the high calling of husband and wife, and the grace of God available to be with them in this vocation. It also needs to be memorable so that its teaching makes its way into the memory and thus into the consciences of those who hear and speak it. This is obviously true of the marriage service in both the 1662 and 1928 *Prayer Books*, even though some modern people do not like their declaration of the sexual weaknesses of human beings or the vow of obedience taken by the woman. What is provided in *Pastoral Services* is certainly a Christian marriage ceremony; but, in that which surrounds the basic solemn declarations and vows it is a text/ceremony without real quality in the contents of its Introduction, Preface, Collect and Prayers at the end. Composing long statements and prayers to be read aloud and which do appropriate honour to God and man, and which make good use of the English language is, as we have said often, a gift which few possess.

Likewise, the Funeral Service needs to be both grave and memorable on the one hand and filled with Christian hope through dramatic but controlled language on the other. After all it is, in the reformed Catholic tradition of the Church of England, meant to be a strong affirmation of the resurrection to eternal life in the society of the redeemed in the kingdom of God, and a committing of the deceased baptized person in faith, hope and love into the everlasting care of the God and Father of our Lord Jesus Christ. The Funeral Services in *Pastoral Services* provide an adequate but not an engaging proclamation of the Christian hope. Further, if all the provisions are taken seriously at the local parish level then the minister will need to take his volume, *Pastoral Services*, everywhere he goes in connection with the events and pastoral visits surrounding a death and funeral service. Happily it has an Index and so it is to be hoped that he will be able to locate what he needs to use efficiently and quickly.

CHAPTER EIGHT

Prayers and Collects

A necessary and essential part of Christian public worship is the addressing of Almighty God, the Father of the Lord Jesus Christ, in prayer. Over the centuries the Church, the people who are called to enjoy and glorify God for ever, have daily worshipped this Almighty Father. To do so they have developed suitably reverential, humble and intelligible forms of words together with an appropriate style in order to fulfil this high vocation of speaking to God in the sanctuary. The form of words used has not been either the lowest or the highest common denominator, but has been of such a kind that most ordinary people after instruction and through habit of use can grasp its meaning, that to which it points and that which it communicates. At the same time the vocabulary and style have been such as to satisfy the educated and those of high culture. There has been the pursuit of excellence in the sense of providing the best form of words and style to provide for the unique purpose of being spoken aloud in public worship and being memorable.

One of the more distinctive parts of both the medieval Latin Missal and English Common Prayer is that form of prayer, always one sentence, known as "the collect" (Latin, *collecta* and *oratio*). In the Latin Mass, the collect made its appearance in the second half of the fifth century and was constructed within the conventions of the classical Roman and Latin rhetorical tradition. It became the first distinctly priestly prayer of the mass and served both to conclude the entrance rite and to introduce the reading of the Epistle and Gospel. Further, by its content it often announced a particular festival or theme. The *Sarum Missal*, which Archbishop Cranmer used as a young priest, contained many such collects for Sundays, Festivals, Holy Days, and Commemorations of Saints. *Collect* is a word descending by two routes from Latin, meaning in the one "a prayer of the collected people" and in the other "a prayer collecting the thoughts of the day". Cranmer was aware of both meanings and especially the second which spoke to him of the need for clear, well-constructed prayers, suitable for use in public worship. So it is not surprising that in the English *Book of the Common Prayer* (1549), of which he was the major architect, the collect not only retained its unique place before the Epistle and Gospel but also displayed a style and characteristics that soon made it a most memorable part of the English Liturgy. Further, other prayers, similar in structure but different in content, were created by him for use in the major public services and these are often also in English referred to as collects. The best known of these include the Collect for Purity in Holy Communion, the Collects for Peace at the end of Morning and Evening Prayer and the Collects at the end of the Litany.

Of Archbishop Thomas Cranmer's work in producing the English Liturgy, Professor E. C. Ratcliff wrote:

> Cranmer was the master, or rather the creator, of English liturgical style, because he had apprehended the nature of worship. To serve the purposes of worship he brought the resources of the scholar: appreciation of the fine compositions of liturgical Latin; knowledge of the rules of rhythm and clausula; facility and felicity in translation; a feeling for the wonder of words. With such resources, and moved by a profound religious sincerity, Cranmer made of English a liturgical language comparable with Latin at its best. "The ink of the scholar," so runs an Arabic proverb, "is of more worth than the blood of a martyr." The proverb is true of Cranmer. In his liturgy he bequeathed to the newly reformed Church of England an instrument of life, and which also, in its remarkable combination of the traditional with the contemporary, of the old with the new, was to be not the least important factor in imparting to Anglican Christianity its distinctive stamp.[1]

Cranmer did his translating and composing in order to produce prayers to be read aloud. The challenge before him was to reproduce in English the complicated syntax of a Latin sentence and at the same time make it both pleasant to hear and worthy of being committed to memory. He succeeded, and millions of every social class and educational background have benefited from that success over the centuries.[2]

The English Collect

The Collect is a one-sentence prayer which in its fullest expression has five parts, but which may only have three (the first, third and fifth below). First comes the Invocation or Address, usually to the Father of our Lord Jesus Christ, but occasionally to the Lord Jesus himself

1 E. C. Ratcliff, *Liturgical Studies*, 1976, p. 199

2 See further Ian Robinson, *The Establishment of Modern English Prose in the Reformation and the Enlightenment*, Cambridge, 1998.

and once to the Blessed Trinity. In the second place, there is the Recital and Remembrance of some doctrine or biblical fact, by means of a relative clause. Thirdly, the Petition or Request, which constitutes the body of the prayer and uses the first person plural (*us* or *our*). In the fourth place the Aspiration or devout wish, expressing a purpose of the petition. Finally, there is the Pleading of the Name of Jesus the Mediator when the prayer is addressed to the Father, and a doxology when addressed to the Son or the Holy Trinity.

In the Recital or Remembrance (which we may also call the Commemoration) Cranmer consistently followed the *Deus qui* of his originals and made constant use of the relative clause. For example for Christmas Day he provided, "Almighty God, who hast given us thy only-begotten Son to take our nature upon him, and as at this time to be born of a pure Virgin: Grant ... ." Here we see the Invocation to the Father, the Recital by means of a relative clause, "who hast given ... ", and the beginning of the Petition. Let us focus on the use of the relative clause. It is skilfully constructed both here and in 44 other collects in the original 1549 *Prayer Book* in order to preserve the mood of reverence and recollection as God's people engage in active remembrance of one or another aspect of God's revelation to men. If it had been third person singular, "who has given us his only-begotten Son", then it would have ceased to be prayerful meditation before God and have become a kind of aside to oneself or those near to one. The use of the second person singular seeks to ensure the flow and continuity of the prayer as an address to God the Father; and the use of the relative avoids the suggestion that the recital, remembrance and commemoration is in the mind of God and not in ours.

Here is another example to help clarify the matter. The Collect for The Epiphany begins: "O God, who by the leading of a star didst manifest thy only-begotten Son to the Gentiles: Mercifully grant that we ... ." First there is the Invocation or Address to the Father of the incarnate Son, next the relative clause, and then the Petition. If the text had "did manifest his only-begotten Son" it would be third person singular, and the meaning would be that the priest offering the prayer was ceasing to address God while he said a few words to himself or to those listening to him. The use of the second person singular in the relative clause ensures that the information is prayerful meditation and not a public announcement.

It may seem that we are labouring the point. Perhaps we are. However, to make it as clear as possible is necessary today if we are to understand and appreciate the particular nature of English Common Prayer and of the unique function within it of the collect.

After all we do live in days when few people seem to have been taught the basics of grammar and syntax in their study of the English language at school; so talk in the church of first person and second person as well as relative clauses is as a foreign tongue to many or as computer language is to the elderly. In fact, it is partly because of a general decline amongst English-speaking people of a knowledge of basic grammar that the Liturgical Commission of the late 1970s decided to modify the structure and style of collects which were put into *The Alternative Service Book 1980*. Thus, according to the Liturgical Commission of 2000,

> The *A[lternative] S[ervice] B[ook]* significantly reshaped the language, function, and traditional reference points [as they had been known in the *Prayer Book*] of the collects. Simpler, contemporary language replaced the latinate Cranmerian style, and the relative clause containing an attribute of God gave way (often with unfortunate results) to a statement about God.[1]

Also, the association of familiar collects with particular Sundays was often lost in the 1980 production because of the decision to make the collect serve the purpose of introducing the appointed, thematic Bible readings for that day.

Common Worship sought to correct the admitted errors and excesses of its predecessor of two decades earlier by restoring in many cases the relative clause and also by producing a full set of collects in traditional language to accompany those services which use this idiom. Further, the doxological, Trinitarian, longer ending is mandatory for Sundays and major holy days—"who is alive and reigns with you [O Father], in the unity of the Holy Spirit, one God, now and for ever". Here the provision of the *Prayer Book* is much exceeded, which wisely reserved the full Trinitarian ending primarily for major Festivals—Christmas, Easter, Ascension and Whitsunday—so that it would be heard and recognized as very special indeed. Then, also, *Common Worship* provides (as did the Latin Mass and the 1549 *Prayer Book*) Post-Communion Prayers, having a structure similar to the collect. These prayers "acknowledge feast days and seasons in their intentions" but "again and again, they are eschatological, reminding worshippers that it is through participation in the Eucharist that we are offered a foretaste of the heavenly banquet."[2]

It appears that the present Liturgical Commission and General Synod face a crisis about this unique form of prayer, the collect. They have tried to do better than their predecessors in the 1970s by drawing nearer to the classic tradition of English Common Prayer and by using the relative clause. However, they believed it was right

---

1 *Companion*, p. 181   2 *Ibid.*, p. 183

or necessary sometimes to retain the 1970s innovation of the declarative main clause in which God is seemingly told what he already knows. This mixed effort sent forth mixed signals into the church and world and has not met with the general approval expected and hoped for from all quarters.

Some people were unhappy either with the recovery of the relative clause or the use of the declarative clause. One letter in the *Church Times*, from Dr Ross Hutchison, claimed that "about half the collects [in the main volume] use distorted and unnatural English, while about 30 per cent use jargon. Advent 2 is perhaps the most extreme case."[1] So what is provided for the Second Sunday of Advent?

> O Lord, raise up, we pray, your power
> and come among us,
> and with great might succour us;
> that whereas, through our sins and wickedness
> we are grievously hindered
> in running the race that is set before us,
> your bountiful grace and mercy
> may speedily help and deliver us;
> through Jesus Christ your Son our Lord,
> to whom with you and the Holy Spirit,
> be honour and glory, now and for ever.

This, no doubt, is seen an example of "distorted and unnatural English" rather than jargon. It is certainly not the easiest of the collects either to read or to understand, because of the awkward "that whereas ... ." It is best encountered in its original Latin form or in its 1549 English rendering.[2]

Demands increased for radically new and simplified collects. A consultation exercise undertaken by the Liturgical Commission in 2002 produced a wide range of criticisms of the collects in *Common Worship*. The most common were:—The syntax of them is too complicated and archaic; they are too long; they are bland in the themes, imagery and choice of language which they use ("they end up saying very little, and take a long time to say it, in an unnecessarily complicated way"); the closing doxology adds to their complexity and length, and their language is frequently inaccessible for certain contexts; for example, where children are present in significant numbers, in "non-book" contexts, and among missionary congregations where there is no background experience of the language of *The Book of Common Prayer*.

1 21 February 2003

2 The original Latin form of this collect is for Advent 1 in the Sarum Missal while in the 1549 and 1662 *Prayer Book* it is for Advent 4. The present collect is an attempt to put into "contemporary English" the "traditional language" of the 1662 collect at the same time as omitting the reference in 1662 to "the satisfaction of" Jesus Christ.

To meet this barrage of criticism, which the Commission apparently took very seriously, it was decided that a whole new alternative set of collects must be composed—short, simple in their syntax, vivid and interesting in their themes and imagery, accessible in the kind of language they use, and which end up by saying something clear and distinct. The Commission decided upon the following Guidelines:—

1 The collects are, in general, to be significantly shorter than those contained in *Common Worship*;

2 On the occasions when the relative clause is used, attention is to be paid to the need for brevity;

3 Use of the vocative form "O God ... " is to be avoided;

4 Use of archaisms in both syntax and language is to be rigorously avoided;

5 Use of a closing Trinitarian doxology is to be dropped except in a few significant cases, but in a number of instances an essentially Trinitarian framework will govern the structure of the prayer;

6 Contemporary imagery and directness of language are to be adopted in many cases, without the concomitant pitfall of being so over-direct that the prayer fails to apply "across the board" and so to perform its function of "collecting" the prayers of all the people; and

7 When direct language is used, sermonizing or moralizing in the prayer is to be avoided.

The result was that in February 2003, as was noted in Chapter Three, the Liturgical Commission placed before the General Synod another set of collects, *Common Worship: Additional Collects*, to provide an alternative to those already authorised. The new set is intended to be as simple as possible and in being so it runs the serious risk of providing an outstanding example of dumbing down within the official liturgy of a national Church that has such a fine history of the pursuit of excellence in words and music in the service of God.

In Chapter Three we looked at several examples of the latest simplified collects and it will be useful now to look at more. Here are those for Ash Wednesday and the First Sunday of Lent:

God the only saviour,
our lives are laid open before you:
help us to turn to you this Lent,
and through your Son,
the skilful healer,
strengthen us and make us whole
in the power of the Holy Spirit.

Heavenly Father,
your Son battled with the powers of darkness,

and grew closer to you in the desert:
help us to use these days to grow in wisdom and prayer
that we may witness to your saving love
in Jesus Christ our Lord.

The first one does not address God as "O God" but directly as "God" which sounds strange to English ears. There is no logical connection between his being the "only saviour" and the fact that we tell him that "our lives are open before you". Then the petition "help us to turn to you this Lent" is a strange request for we should be turned to God all the time and be asking here for special Lenten grace. Finally, the collect has no ending or termination normal in prayer addressed to the Father. Possibly the reason for this is the use of "through your Son" as part of the petition for strengthening and being made whole. In the second one, Jesus is made to appear like one of us when he is said to have "grown closer to you (God) in the desert." He was in intimate communion when he went into the desert, through the testing, and when he left. It is we, who are sinners, who by grace may grow closer. Also, there is no proper ending, probably because the "in Jesus Christ" which is an extension of "saving love" is treated as if it were the actual ending. The general impression made by these and the rest of this collection is that they were composed either by novices or by those who were on a determined mission to dumb down this most ancient western form of prayer called the collect.

The style and theological content of these new prayers raise serious questions about what is happening within the Liturgical Commission, the General Synod and the Church of England. Not too long ago, this Church possessed in the collects of the *Prayer Book* a treasury of prayer and practical doctrine that was very widely appreciated and admired. Now the same Church does not seem to know where to go next to find within the new idiom of contemporary language suitable replacements for the old collects in their traditional language of prayer.

Another letter in the 21 February 2003 issue of the *Church Times*, from Dr Alistair MacGregor, makes a claim concerning the unity of a true collect.

A collect presents a sequence of ideas unifying the entire prayer, in which the parts are so skilfully blended that the joints do not protrude. The relative clause is a vital element that helps to preserve the unity of the prayer. It sustains the predicative attributes of God, and thus anticipates the remainder of the prayer. Remove the relative pronoun and substitute a main clause for the relative clause, and the prayer loses its cohesion and flow and falls flat. A declarative statement at the beginning of a collect inevitably detracts from the petitionary imperative at its heart.

Here we have a description of a perfect medieval Latin or Cranmerian collect with a warning of how not to change it.

The Collect for Christmas Day in the *Prayer Book* (noted above) fits the bill but that in *Common Worship* "loses its cohesion and flow and falls flat on its face":

> Almighty God,
> you have given us your only-begotten Son
> to take our nature upon him
> and as at this time to be born of a pure virgin:
> grant that we, who have been born again ...

This could have begun, "Almighty God, who have given us ... " but the relative pronoun has been removed and a main clause has been substituted. And God is being told of what he has done for us in his only-begotten Son, and perhaps we expect a reply from him like, "Oh yes I did so. Thanks for reminding me." The creators of the Collect for Christmas Eve make the same mistake as for Christmas Day. Instead of beginning, "Almighty God, who make us glad ... " we are given:

> Almighty God,
> you make us glad with the yearly remembrance
>   of the birth of your Son Jesus Christ:
> grant that, as we joyfully receive him as our redeemer ...

Again it all falls flat on its face, as do the whole of the nineteen collects that have this structure. Although not tried in *Common Worship*, it is possible to begin a collect with, "Almighty God, you who ... ". It has been observed that there is no grammatical or stylistic reason why a contemporary version of the *Agnus Dei* should not begin, "O Lamb of God, you who take away the sin of the world, have mercy upon us." Apparently "you who" is commonplace in novels and on the stage and so would not be out of place in contemporary liturgical English. However, there seems to be a widely held feeling, perhaps conviction, that in "contemporary liturgical language" the use of the relative clause and "you who" sound odd and should be avoided. If this is so, then the question arises whether new collects that are worthy of being used publicly can actually be written today! However, amongst all the extremely numerous options within *Common Worship* the use of the *Prayer Book* collects is not one. Any church that decides to take the simplest route out of this maze will have to use the *Prayer Book*, its collects and its lectionary.

Be that as it may, the new set of simplified collects is soon to be made available, and it is likely that some both in the main set and the subsidiary set will sooner or later be revised or rewritten. There is, therefore, confusion as to what is the collect and whether it is really necessary any more to have it with the Bible readings when the liturgy is much more flexible. At the moment it is seen as part of the invariable shape but perhaps it will soon cease to be so and become only one of the possible ingredients.

Post-Communion Prayers

It is not clear whether the criticisms levelled against the collects also applied to the Post-Communion Prayers, for some of them do use the relative clause and others the declarative clause. Since the Post-Communion Prayers are only used at the Eucharist, even though they are as plentiful in numbers as the former, they are used less and so make less impact. Nevertheless they are prayers and as such, if the law of praying is the law of believing, then what they contain is to be taken seriously. Their quality, shape and ingredients vary tremendously even though it is claimed that a major theme in many of them is the Christian hope of being with the redeemed at the heavenly banquet of the Lord in the age to come.

The prayer for Advent 1 is based on that in the Gelasian Sacramentary and is thematically linked with the collect in the images of watchfulness and wakefulness:

> O Lord our God,
> make us watchful and keep us faithful
> as we await the coming of your Son our Lord;
> that, when he shall appear,
> he may not find us sleeping in sin
> but active in his service
> and joyful in his praise;
> through Jesus Christ our Lord.

One cannot find major fault with this, but that for Advent 3 is open to serious criticism:

> We give you thanks, O Lord, for these heavenly gifts;
> kindle in us the fire of your Spirit
> that when your Christ comes again
> we may shine as lights before his face;
> who is alive and reigns now and for ever.

It is not clear what are "these heavenly gifts". Perhaps they are the sacramental bread and wine or perhaps (from the Collect for the Day) the gifts of ministry. The relation between kindling a fire and shining as lights is strained, for while a fire gives light it primarily burns and is hot. Then the last line is a poor way to end a prayer, for while it speaks of God's Christ as alive and reigning it does not establish his role as Mediator, that we plead and pray in his Name. It could have been "through him who is alive and reigns now and forever" as in other places.

The Annunciation of our Lord (25 March) is a Principal Feast and the Collect is sound and based on that in the *Prayer Book*, but with the longer, Trinitarian ending. In contrast, the Post-Communion Prayer is entirely new and most daring in its use of images.

> God most high,
> whose handmaid bore the Word made flesh:
> we thank you that in this sacrament of our redemption
> you visit us with your Holy Spirit
> and overshadow us by your power;
> strengthen us to walk with Mary the joyful path of obedience
> and so to bring forth the fruits of holiness;
> through Jesus Christ our Lord.

Whether it is right to begin "God" rather than "O God" we pass by, to ask whether it is appropriate or even reverent to use of Christians the image/words addressed to the Blessed Virgin at a unique moment in her life and in the redeeming acts of God. The angel said to Mary, "The Holy Spirit will come upon you, and the power of the Most High will overshadow you; therefore the child to be born will be called holy, the Son of God" (RSV, Luke 1: 35). This statement both points to the miraculous conception by Mary of the one to be called Jesus and to the first moment of Incarnation of the Son of God, taking flesh in the virgin's womb. The uniqueness of the event makes it inappropriate for use in a general way. Here is a bright idea gone wrong.

Other Prayers

Apart from Collects, Post-Communion Prayers and Eucharistic Prayers, there are in the main volume other forms of prayer, notably the Litany, Thanksgivings for use at Morning and Evening Prayer, Prayers for Various Occasions, Authorized Forms of Confession and various other optional prayers.

One of the first things one notices, if one is familiar with the *Prayer Book*, is that it is possible to use *Common Worship* and, apparently, never pray for the Queen, who has a unique relation to the Church of England as its supreme governor. Apparently it is not part of the required ingredients, not even on Sundays, that there be intercessions for the Queen or the Royal Family. This is very odd and may be an over-reaction against the *Prayer Book*, where repeated and required intercession is made for the monarch. Prayers for the Sovereign, the Royal Family and Those who Govern are certainly provided in "Prayers for Various Occasions"[1] from which one or more may be [not "must be"] selected for use in the Intercessions before the end of Morning or Evening Prayer. Happily none of these collects includes a declarative clause telling the Most High Sovereign and King of kings what he already knows about this English monarch! But in the "Additional Collects" in this section four out of the nine provided make use of the declarative instead of the relative clause in the addressing of God and end up telling the Almighty and Omniscient Father some very basic information about his ways and deeds. It is also of note that there is no prayer anywhere to be prayed in time of war (this is written as the War against Iraq proceeds).

The new Litany,[2] which does, happily, allow prayer for the monarch, is stripped down to the bare essential petititions and responses and presents human beings before God who are apparently less conscious of their sinfulness than those who use the old Litany. Section 1 uses both the minimum number of words to address the Three Persons of the Holy Trinity and to ask for mercy. For example, "Holy, blessed and glorious Trinity" is used instead of "O holy, blessed and glorious Trinity, three Persons and one God" and thus an opportunity to express right doctrine to God is lost. In the response "Have mercy upon us" replaces the full naming of the Holy Trinity followed by " ... have mercy upon us, miserable sinners." No one enjoys being described as a miserable sinner but if this is what we are before the holy Lord our God then this is what we must call ourselves (miserable = wretchedly needy).

The Authorized Forms of Confession and Absolution[3] like the Litany deal with sinfulness as though it were less than the devastating and disastrous spiritual disease and cancer that it is. The general tenor and content of the confessions to God lack the appropriate element of seriousness expressed in carefully chosen vocabulary and phraseology. They give the impression that the way to forgiveness is a reasonably trouble-free route not needing profound self-examination and penitence. And virtually all the Absolutions begin with "May ..." thus giving the impression of probability rather than certainty, or perhaps communicating the idea that since sin is serious but not all that devastating, a sure word of forgiveness is not wholly required.

The form of Confession suggested for Christmas time is a brief Litany where the people respond, "Forgive and heal us" after a statement has been made to the "Lord of grace and truth". Thus we have:

> The Virgin Mary accepted your call
> to be the mother of Jesus.
> Forgive our disobedience to your will.

1 *Common Worship*, pp. 101ff.   2 pp. 111–14   3 pp. 122ff.

We have sinned:

All   **forgive and heal us.**

Your Son our Saviour
was born in poverty in a manger.
Forgive our greed and rejection of your ways.
We have sinned:

All   **forgive and heal us.**

The shepherds left their flocks
to go to Bethlehem.
Forgive our self-interest and lack of vision.
We have sinned:

All   **forgive and heal us.**[1]

This has the appearance of being put together by someone who was given the task (in committee) of relating well-known facts about Christmas to confessing sins. Not only is it not real prayer to a living, holy God, but also it has factual errors (Jesus was not born in a manger but placed in one after being born) and the connection of the information given to God and the confession made to him is a very weak one at best. How can genuinely contrite and repentant people pray this kind of prayer without feeling embarrassed and humiliated?

The Forms of Intercession[2] for use at Holy Communion that are not from the *Prayer Book* are, like the Litany, trimmed down to basics and have a somewhat staccato effect because of their brevity of expression and the way their petitions follow on from each other— asking/telling God to Strengthen, Bless, Guide, Give grace to, Comfort, Heal and so on. They are very much designed for the modern happy situation where a lay person takes the lead and the assembled people respond or are allowed to make additions or name names. Further, they are designed to be followed by a collect said by the Celebrant. Of the eight endings (collects) provided, four have a declarative clause, one (from the *Prayer Book*) has the relative clause, and the others are direct petitions without any remembrance before God or declaration to him at the beginning of the prayer.

Conclusion

If there is one area of human life where an assembly of Christian people ought to excel at offering their best to God it is in prayer, in the daring exercise where mortal, feeble man addresses (and expects to be heard by) the immortal, omnipotent LORD God. In private prayer each person is personally responsible for himself before his

1 p. 123   2 pp. 281ff.

Creator and Redeemer, but in public worship, what is addressed to the Almighty LORD our God is addressed on behalf of all present (and in fact sometimes on behalf of the whole creation). The meaningful words, phrases and sentences reverently and humbly offered have to speak on behalf of all and thus must be in a form and style that fulfils the dual purpose both of adequately representing all present and also of representing these adopted children of God as they address their heavenly Father, who is also their Creator, Redeemer and Judge. Obviously here the language of the street or of the media show will hardly suffice, for we are not dealing with people saying "Hi, John! How are you?" to each other. No, we are dealing with finite, weak creatures, wholly dependent upon their Creator and Sustainer, who are speaking collectively to this personal Deity, who is their heavenly Father.

So it is not surprising that the Church has developed and cultivated ways of addressing the God and Father of the Lord Jesus Christ, and it is foolish, perhaps arrogant, not to use them or be guided by them today. Simplifying and dumbing down do not work, for they speak in the end for no-one, being merely the propaganda tools of those who sincerely desire to change radically the relation of man to God, thinking that ordinary folks cannot raise their eyes and voices towards heaven, when they use a form of words hallowed by tradition over centuries of prayerful use. It is worth recalling that millions of ordinary people learned off by heart the prayers/collects of *The Book of Common Prayer* and found them to be in the changing circumstances and challenges of life their own real prayer to God.

CHAPTER NINE

Bible and Doctrine

Apologists for the Church of England at the end of the Elizabethan period invented a simple way to state and remember the doctrinal foundation if the Church of England as a national church and a jurisdiction of the one, holy, catholic and apostolic Church of God the Father. They said that is was built upon *One* canon of Holy Scripture made up of *Two* Testaments, whose central witness and teaching is summarised in *Three* Creeds (Apostles', Nicene & Athanasian), whose basic dogma is set forth by the first *Four* Ecumenical Councils (Nicea [325], Constantinople [381], Ephesus [431] & Chalcedon [451]) and whose worship, ministry and general life is based on *Five* centuries of history and experience. Because of this kind of apology, the curriculum for theological students up to the 1960s was dominated by studies of Scripture and the Early Church to A.D. 500. It was further argued that the Formularies of the Church of England, the *Prayer Book*, the Articles of Religion and the Ordinal conformed to this general pattern, in which the primacy and authority of Scripture is clear. Yet this is Scripture in the context of the Church, the Household of God, not Scripture standing alone, and further the Church of England traditionally emphasizes the logic of beginning with the whole of Scripture as given by God and then seeing it as made up of two testaments. In modern universities the departments of Old and New Testament Studies are usually separated not only spatially but also in terms of method. Thus few students come away with a sense of the primary unity of Scripture. Rather, they come away with questions as to the relation of the two Testaments, and in particular, the Messianic and Christological interpretation of the Old Testament.

Canon A5 states the current doctrinal basis of the Church of England:

> The doctrine of the Church of England is grounded in the Holy Scriptures, and in such teachings of the ancient Fathers and Councils of the Church as are agreeable to the said Scriptures. In particular such doctrine is to be found in the Thirty-nine Articles of Religion, *The Book of Common Prayer*, and the Ordinal.

This canon is based on The Worship and Doctrine Measure, 1974, Section 5(1), and it is under this Measure that alternative forms of service to those in *The Book of Common Prayer* have been authorised.

The Bible

It has been widely acknowledged that the historic Liturgy of the Church of England is scriptural. Not only does it include large portions of the Bible (Epistle, Gospel, Canticles, Versicles and Psalter) but also there is the rich and varied use of scriptural language, images, citations, and doctrines in the litany, prayers, collects, commandments, exhortations, and absolutions. Happily this has been documented in great detail by Henry Ives Bailey, Vicar of North Leverton, near Retford, Nottinghamshire.[1] In an Appendix his book also contains a List of all the direct quotations from the Bible in the *Prayer Book*. Further, the official Lectionaries (i.e., those of 1662, 1871 & 1922) that go with the *Prayer Book* and associated with the weekday and Sunday services provide a more than adequate coverage of the whole Bible.

In the writing of modern liturgies the close and intimate ties with the language of the Bible have not been maintained. One reason for this is that there is an excessive number of modern versions of the Bible and thus no one of them is sufficiently well known to be quoted or cited. Another reason is that the desire to create gender inclusive language, as it is called, makes the relation to the ancient Bible problematic. But, probably the major reason is that modern liturgical scholars do not live in the world and text of the Bible as did Archbishop Cranmer and his colleagues. They do not know the content and text of the Bible as well as did the sixteenth century churchmen and so in their writing the allusions, citations and quotations do not flow so easily or richly as they did for Cranmer.[2]

If one combed through the main services of *The Alternative Service Book* and *Common Worship* one would not be able to write a book such as Bailey wrote because the new liturgies cannot be realistically compared with the Bible by the use of parallel columns. They are not scriptural in a direct sense for they do not often weave biblical phrases and texts into the prayer or exhortation or address. In truth they are, as it were, in most of their content, one remove from the Bible. The relation is general rather than specific. Take for example this extract from Prayer D, newly composed for Order One, the Holy

---

1 H. I. Bailey, *The Liturgy compared with the Bible, or an illustration and confirmation by Scripture quotations and references of such parts of The Book of Common Prayer ... as are not direct extracts from the Holy Scriptures*, SPCK, 778 pp., first published 1833 and often reprinted

2 For Cranmer's attitude to the Bible see his original preface for the 1549 *Prayer Book* entitled in the 1662 *Prayer Book* "Concerning the Service of the Church", and the first Homily on the "Reading of Holy Scripture" in *The First Book of Homilies* (1547).

Communion of *Common Worship*:

> Almighty God, good Father to us all,
> your face is turned towards your world.
> In love you gave us Jesus your Son
> to rescue us from sin and death.
> Your Word goes out to call us home
>   to the city where angels sing your praise.

Whatever may be the theological and devotional merit of these sentences, placed between the Sursum Corda and the Sanctus, it would be difficult to line up alongside them verses from the New Revised Standard Version, for example, to show their direct relation to a prominent English version of Holy Scripture favoured by the Liturgical Commission. Where can we find a direct parallel to "good Father to us all" and where do we read in the Bible that God's face is turned towards the world? Then, though it is said that God's face is turned towards the world, it is only to "us" not the world as world that he gave Jesus. The use of the upper case for "Word" suggests that the Son of God rather than the spoken word of God is intended. But in the Prologue of the Gospel according to St John, the Word "became flesh and dwelt among us." He did so to save us from the wrath of God and draw us into communion with the Father and the Son, a communion which is both for this age and the age to come, and into a communal life that embraces all the children of God. The association of the Logos with "the city" (= the Jerusalem which is above) is far from clear. The relation of Eucharistic Prayer to Scripture here is at best indirect.

Nevertheless, one can be misled into supposing that within the texts of *Common Worship: Services and Prayers* an index to actual biblical references can be found, for in the main volume from page 823 to page 836 (some 14 pages) there is what is called "Index of Biblical References". However, this is primarily and nearly exclusively an index of the Lectionary found on pages 537–90. Therefore, even if it does not tell us how the Bible is used in the text of the Liturgy it does provide a most useful source to check which parts of the Bible are *not* read on Sundays and principal feast days. One such omission is Romans 1: 18ff., which is a major statement concerning God's wrath against ungodliness and unrighteousness, including sodomy.

One further comment is appropriate with respect to the general relation of *Common Worship* to the Bible, and this concerns what we have come to call Bible Sunday. In the *Prayer Book*, the place of the Bible in the Church of God is celebrated on the Second Sunday in Advent, at the very beginning of the Christian Year. For this day the well-known Collect written by Archbishop Cranmer is used: "Blessed Lord, who hast caused all Holy Scripture to be written for our learning ... ." In *Common Worship* Bible Sunday is the Last Sunday after Trinity, the end of the Christian Year. Here symbolism, it could be said, speaks louder than words.

One book of the Bible was especially translated for *Common Worship*: the Psalter. This is the one book of the Bible that is used daily at both Morning and Evening Prayer, as well as at Compline. Its importance in the life of the Church and Christian people is clear. The new Psalter

> differs from any Psalter previously printed in Church of England service books, and yet is closely related to them. It is cast in "you" form language, is generally inclusive of men and women, attends to the worshipping traditions which have shaped the Church of England, is rhythmic, is reasonably accessible to a wide range of worshippers and falls within the parameters of contemporary Hebrew scholarship.[1]

Significantly, it is *not* claimed that this Psalter can be *prayed* in the way in which the Church has traditionally prayed the Psalter over the centuries in the daily offices, that is, with a full messianic and christological understanding and insight. This is how the Introduction to *The Divine Office* of the Roman Catholic Church stated this approach:

> Whoever says the Psalms in the name of the Church should pay attention to the full meaning of the Psalms, especially the messianic understanding which led the Church to adopt the Psalter. The messianic meaning is made completely manifest in the New Testament; it is in fact declared by Christ our Lord. ... Following this path, the Fathers took the whole Psalter and explained it as a prophecy about Christ and his Church; and for this same reason psalms were chosen for the sacred liturgy. Even if certain artificial interpretations were sometimes accepted, generally both the Fathers and the liturgy rightly heard in the Psalms Christ calling out to his Father, or the Father speaking to the Son; they even recognized in them the voice of the Church, the apostles and martyrs. ... This christological interpretation in no way refers only to those psalms which are considered messianic but also extends to many in which without doubt there are mere appropriations. Such appropriations, however, have been commended by the tradition of the Church.

In his *Ennarations* upon the Psalms, Bishop Augustine of Hippo uses the christological interpretation to powerful effect. One of his finest expositions of the logic of the christological approach is found in his comments on Psalm 86: "We pray to him [Jesus], through him, in him; and we speak with him, and he speaks with us; we speak in him, he speaks in us the prayer of this Psalm, which is entitled 'A Prayer of David'." This approach to the Psalter is well expressed in a

1 *Companion*, p. 238

simplified form in the Preface to the much-used devotional *Commentary on the Psalms* (1836) by George Horne, Bishop of Norwich. It is found in richness in the Neale and Littledale *Commentary on the Psalter* in four volumes.[1] In more recent times it was embraced by Dietrich Bonhoeffer, the opponent of Hitler's régime in Germany, when he was Director of the seminary of the Confessing Church. His book *Das Gebetbuch der Bibel* (1940) has been translated as *The Psalms: Prayer Book of the Bible*,[2] and shows how the Christological can be married to the historical, literary approach.

The traditional meditatory and christological use of the Psalms has been made nearly impossible today in Anglican public worship by at least two basic causes. First, the emphasis in modern Biblical Studies is to ascertain who wrote the Psalms, when, for whom, in what context and for what purpose. This can be a fascinating study but runs the risk of merely making one an expert in ancient religion and practice and with little or no ear for the patristic way of using the Psalter or for its use as the primary Christian Prayer Book. In the second place, because of the success of the feminist movement, most modern translations or paraphrases seek to exclude as far as possible what in our era is perceived as the patriarchal, androcentric and sexist emphasis of the original composers of the Psalms, king David and his allies. This unwanted emphasis and orientation is removed surgically and practically by the use of "inclusive language", which method is used in the Psalter of *Common Worship* in three ways: changing the Hebrew third person masculine singular pronoun to the first person singular or to impersonal or plural pronouns; the use of abstract nouns; and the use of generic terms such as "mortals" and "humanity".

One need only look at the first verse of the first Psalm to see how, from the viewpoint of the Church in days past, Jesus Christ has been excluded from the very Psalter that was his basic prayer book and from which he used prayers at critical moments in his life and ministry. The *Prayer Book* has, "Blessed is the man that hath not walked in the counsel of the ungodly ... ." "Man" here has for centuries been taken to refer prophetically to "the Man, Christ Jesus" who is the new Adam. And the Psalm has been taken as introducing the whole Psalter, with the result that Jesus is here established as the One to whom the whole Psalter witnesses. In total contrast Psalm 1 in *Common Worship* uses one of its three means to make the masculine singular into an inclusive form, here an impersonal plural pronoun, "they". Thus "Blessed are they who have not walked in the counsel of the wicked ... ." Yet there is no doubt

---

1 Recently reprinted in the USA by the Lancelot Andrewes Press
2 *The Psalms: Prayer Book of the Bible*, Fairacres, Oxford, 1982

that the original Hebrew word in verse 1 is the word for the male human being, the man, not mankind.[1]

It will be instructive to look at what explanation is offered in the most widely used commentary on the *Prayer Book* in the late nineteenth and early twentieth century, *The Annotated Prayer Book* by Canon J. H. Blunt. Here is part of his comment on the meaning of Psalm 1:

> Beyond the obvious moral meaning of this Psalm, it contains a prophetic laudation of the holiness of Christ. He is "the Man" to whom we sing, "Blessing, and glory, and wisdom, and thanksgiving, and honour, and power, and might" as the Lamb of God who is God, throughout the Psalms.
>
> In this particular Psalm he is praised as the only one wearer of our nature in whom pure and perfect holiness has been found during the time of earthly sojourn and probation. In his Temptation, he walked not in the counsel of the Wicked One, stood not in the way of sinners by yielding thereto, and refused the temporal cathedra [throne] which was offered him (though it seemed to bring him in a moment that sovereignty which could otherwise only be won through suffering), because it was the throne of the Evil One, the Prince of this world, and not the throne of the Cross.
>
> His delight was to do the will of Him that sent him, in the day when there was glad sunshine and time to work, and in the night too, when all was eclipse, and darkness and sorrow. Being made perfect through suffering, he became the origin of perfection in others; the Corn of wheat cast into the ground to die and to spring up again with a power of life-giving in its own resurrection; the Corn and Wine of the Tree of Life, planted by that River the streams whereof make glad the City of God; a fruit of sacramental life for the regeneration, edification and resurrection of souls. Nor can any of his work fail through any deficiency of its own; for whatsoever he doeth, whether of grace towards men, or of intercession towards God, it shall prosper, because it is his.
>
> As for The Ungodly who sets up his kingdom against that of Christ, opposing him first by the Jews, then by the heathen, and at all times by sin, the end will prove how great the contrast. The Wind of Pentecost will at least scatter altogether all the opponents of the Kingdom of God, as it has been doing in part ever since its first sound was heard. For them there will be no defence in the dreadful Day of Judgement, nor any place in the Communion of glorified saints. Only the path which he has marked out, who said, "I am the way," can lead to the Presence of God; and they who go in the path of the adversary must take their lot with him.

1 Latin *vir* not *homo*; Greek *aner* not *anthropos*. On Christ and the Psalter see further: Patrick H. Reardon, "Christology and the Psalter: the Church's Christian Prayer Book", in *Creed & Culture*, ed. James H. Kushiner, Wilmington, Delaware, 2003.

> Blessed is the follower of the Man Christ Jesus, who walks in his way, and endureth temptation with steadfastness; for after his trial and victory he also shall receive a crown of life, which the Lord Jesus, the righteous Judge, hath prepared for them that love him, that they may reign with him in glory.[1]

Such doctrinal and devotional thinking and praying is certainly not popular today but it is an authentic way of prayer if the witness of the saints has a vote in what is acceptable. And the point being made here is that it is rendered difficult if not impossible by the inclusivist versions of the Psalter. Those who wish to pray in the traditional way are thus forced to use the Psalter in the *Prayer Book*, in the King James Version, or perhaps *The Revised Psalter* of 1964, in whose creation Professor C. S. Lewis had a significant role.

The favoured translation of the Bible in *Common Worship* is *The New Revised Standard Version* [NRSV] published in 1990. Its origins go back to 1974 when the Policies Committee of the National Council of Churches in the USA authorized the preparation of a revision of the entire *Revised Standard Bible*. The general mandate to the translation team was summed up in the maxim: "As literal as possible, as free as necessary". Specific mandates to the translators included the elimination of masculine-oriented language where, in their opinion, the reference was clearly to both men and women (e. g., "brothers and sisters" for "brethren"). Interestingly, it never seems to have occurred to the participants in this project that the substitution of "brothers and sisters" for the single Greek word translated "brethren" (*adelphoi*) might actually work against Christian equality, since men and women were no longer defined by a single shared word, but broken into separate categories by a phrase (a group of words). Often the inclusiveness desired by feminist theorists was achieved in the NRSV by simply rephrasing the original or by substituting plural for singular forms (e. g., "Happy are those ... " in Psalm 1:1, instead of "Happy is the man ... "). The judgement expressed by advocates of the NRSV that "with notable success the NRSV has tackled the difficult task of making the English text inclusive where the original is not exclusive" is not as theologically neutral as it sounds.

The Preface of the NRSV states its policy about how to address God:

> It will be seen that in the Psalms and other prayers addressed to God the archaic second person singular pronouns (thou, thee, thine) and verb forms (art, hast, hadst) are no longer used. Although some readers may regret this change, it should be pointed out that in the original languages neither the Old Testament nor the New Testament makes any linguistic distinction between addressing a human being and addressing the Deity.

1 *The Annotated Prayer Book*, edition of 1868, p. 318

What goes missing here is any admission that the Biblical languages do, indeed, distinguish between singular and plural pronouns and verbs, or that such distinctions are important both to the meaning of Scripture and to the absolute assertion that God is One.[1] A different sort of thought has required a different sort of language, and thus, this Version has completely abandoned the traditional English idiom of Prayer, and embraced the modern call for inclusiveness.

Before leaving our reflections on the Bible in Liturgy, a few thoughts on the new Lectionary will be in order. The *Common Worship Lectionary* is not identical with but is based upon *The Revised Common Lectionary*, an ecumenical lectionary closely related to the original Roman Catholic Lectionary. Instead of the one-year cycle of the *Prayer Book* or the two-year cycle of *The Alternative Service Book 1980*, this latest Sunday Lectionary is a three-year cycle, providing three readings (Old Testament, Epistle and Gospel) and a psalm for each Sunday. The year 2000–1 began with the third provision, C, but for the Weekday Lectionary, which is a two year cycle, it began with 1. Thus 2003–4 is C and 2. In the *Companion* the following comment is made about the new provisions: "Obviously this [Sunday provision] leads to a greater use of Scripture, and enables more coherent, continuous reading of biblical books."[2] This is a comment one has heard often in the last twenty or thirty years with respect to new Lectionaries and the adding of an Old Testament reading to the Epistle and Gospel of the *Prayer Book* Eucharist Lectionary. In response it can be said that there is no doubt that those who actually follow the Sunday and Daily Lectionaries and read all the Scripture allocated will certainly read through a vast amount of the Bible, which is in principle an excellent thing. Nevertheless, those who follow the original or the revised (1871/1922) Lectionary of *The Book of Common Prayer* read more, much more, of Holy Scripture weekly, monthly and yearly.

This is probably not the right place to examine the hermeneutical and theological principles that underpin or determine both what is included in and what is omitted from the choice of the readings for the new Lectionary, and when they are used. But questions do arise. For example, do modern critical theories about the literary and textual relations of the Gospel to each other determine the choice of Gospel passages? Do modern critical theories about the origins of the Pentateuch determine which parts are read and when? The advantages of the old Lectionaries are clear even if arguable. First, the Eucharistic Lectionary is very ancient and made holy through devotional usage; thus the Church continued to read what she had read for centuries, accumulating insight as she did so. Then, secondly, the Daily

1 See further, Chapter Ten.　2 *Companion,* p. 230

Lectionary read straight through the Bible in a coherent manner, even when this did not fit into the festivals of the Christian Year.

Doctrine

It is surprising that neither in the main volume of *Common Worship* nor, apparently, anywhere else in other volumes are we provided, in either their original form or in a modern rendering, with the text of either the Thirty-Nine Articles, one of the Formularies of the Church of England, or of one of the three Creeds of the Church, the Athanasian Creed (= Quicunque Vult), or of the Catechism of the Church. Since one of the aims of *Common Worship* is to be so comprehensive that one does not need *The Book of Common Prayer*, the omission of these three fundamental doctrinal statements is most serious; without them the Church of England is beginning to be like a ship without a rudder. *Common Worship* refers to The Articles on page xi and to the Athanasian Creed on page 143 of the main volume, but the actual text of them is not included, and one has to go the *Prayer Book* or to some source of historical documents to find them.[1]

It may be asked: Why should we worry about the Athanasian Creed when its opening words identify rejection of right, orthodox belief with everlasting damnation and thereby offend some people? The answer is that this Creed provides the fullest and clearest statements in the Church of the doctrines of the Blessed, Holy and Undivided Trinity and of the Person of Christ and his Incarnation. The services of *Common Worship* are meant to conform to these foundational doctrines, which are also found in shorter form in Articles I, II, III, IV and V of The Thirty-Nine Articles of Religion.

What we learn from both the Articles and the Athanasian Creed is that doctrinal truth matters, and that to express doctrinal truth, carefully chosen words are necessary. Bearing this in mind it is disappointing that in some places in *Common Worship* the expressions used in relation to the Holy Trinity or the Person of Christ are not accurate. This stands in contrast with *The Book of Common Prayer* which was always seen as providing the means not only to worship the Holy Trinity but also of teaching right ways to think of God.

With respect to the doctrine/dogma of the Holy Trinity, for example, *Common Worship* repeatedly uses the formula, "Blessed be God, Father, Son and Holy Spirit: Blessed be God for ever" in both the main volume[2] and in the *Daily Prayer*.[3] The colon suggests the equivalency of what goes before and after it. In the New Testament

---

1 A part of the Athanasian Creed is, however, used on page 145 as a modern confession of faith in the Lord Jesus Christ.

2 E. g., pp. 32, 48 and 50   3 E. g., pp. 185, 209 and 215

the word "God" virtually always means "God the Father" and only rarely means "Deity, Godhead and Divinity"; and this principle also applies in the collects and prayers of the *Prayer Book*. Now in the contexts of *Common Worship* where this novel pattern of words occurs, the initial prayer is addressed to the Father—for example, "Blessed are you, Lord our God, creator and redeemer of all ... ." Then later in the prayer there is reference usually to both the Son and to the Holy Spirit. Finally, after a full stop there occurs this "blessing of God" which is a required ingredient in the structure.

Several questions arise as one relates this wording to the familiar orthodox statements found in classic sources. In this particular formula it may be asked: Is the first "Blessed be God" a reference to the Godhead, wholly possessed by the each of the Three Persons— the Father, the Son and the Holy Spirit? Or does the word "God" go with each of the Names so that the intended meaning is, "Blessed be God the Father, God the Son and God the Holy Spirit"? Is the second use of the word "God" after the colon a reference to God the Father (to whom prayer is usually addressed) or is it to God as the one Divinity, Deity and Godhead wholly present (according to patristic dogma) in each of the Three Persons?

In the modern church environment, where emphasis is upon accessibility, intelligibility and simplicity (even "dumbing-down"), and where not much weight is placed upon the patristic and classical Protestant search for carefully crafted propositional statements of central dogma, such an expression as "God, Father, Son and Holy Spirit" is perhaps deliberately vague. It can be taken to mean that God is One Person with three Modes of being and/or three primary Names. Such a doctrine is by classic standards clearly heresy. It would have been far better to have gone for clarity and accuracy and written, for example, the following. "Blessed be the Father, the Son and the Holy Spirit, one God" with the response, "Blessed be God the Holy Trinity for ever," or another pattern of words that does not leave open the real possibility of understanding God to be One Person with Three Names or Three Expressions of Being. For Unitarianism is more easily embraced by the human mind than is Trinitarianism.

The same general points can be made with reference to the ending of a very short confession of faith on page 148. Here there are three statements: "We believe in God the Father ... in God the Son ... in God the Holy Spirit," followed by "We believe in one God; Father, Son and Holy Spirit". Again why does this last statement have the semicolon? To whom or to what does "God" refer? To the Godhead, to the Trinity or to the Father? The final statement could have been, "We believe in one God, the Father, the Son and the Holy Spirit", to avoid all suggestion of God being one Person with three Names.

When we turn to the Collect and Post-Communion [prayer] for Trinity Sunday,[1] the day when the Church should be at her very clearest in terms of praising the One, Blessed, Holy and Undivided Trinity of the Father and the Son and the Holy Ghost, a Trinity in Unity and a Unity in Trinity, we find ourselves disappointed by the Post-Communion:

> Almighty and eternal God,
> you have revealed yourself as Father, Son and Holy Spirit,
> and live and reign in the perfect unity of love:
> hold us firm in this faith,
> that we may know you in all your ways
> and evermore rejoice in your eternal glory,
> who are three Persons yet one God,
> now and for ever.

The first question to face is, To whom is the Collect addressed? Is it "God" meaning "the Holy Trinity" or "God" meaning the "One Godhead/Divinity/Deity"? If God is meant to be the Holy Trinity, then on Trinity Sunday, such would be understandable and acceptable, even if unique as an address. Yet if it is addressed to the Holy Trinity then confusion begins to surface by the content of the first declaratory clause. The "you have revealed yourself as Father, Son and Holy Spirit ... " seems harmless and straightforward, but stands in contrast to the way of revelation of the Holy Trinity to the people of God as found in Scripture and much studied in the Early Church. The Father is the First Person of the Trinity and it is he who creates the universe through his Son, the Logos, and by the Holy Ghost; the Father is also the First Person who sends the Second Person, the Son, to be the Incarnate Logos, living in his manhood and being the Messiah, empowered and led by the presence and power of the Holy Ghost. The way of revelation is that the Father reveals the Son and the Son makes the Father known to man; further, it is in and by the Incarnate Son that the personhood of the Holy Ghost is known. Bearing this in mind, this prayer would have been better had it begun: "Almighty and eternal God who are the Father, the Son and the Holy Spirit, and live and reign in the perfect unity of love ... " (the traditional version uses the relative clause and so could read, "who art the Father, Son and Holy Ghost ... ").

At least it can be said that this English lack of clarity in dogma is not as bad as that in the American Prayer Book of 1979. Here, in a variety of places, this Greeting or Acclamation occurs:

> *Celebrant* Blessed be God: Father, Son and Holy Spirit.
> *People* And blessed be his kingdom, now and for ever.

1 pp. 406–7 and 478–9

The person who composed this was consciously simplifying and at the same time placing in a different context the Blessing given by the priest, holding the Gospel-book, in the Divine Liturgy of the Orthodox Church. The priest says, "Blessed be the kingdom of the Father and of the Son and of the Holy Ghost, now and always, even unto ages of ages." While the words of the Orthodox liturgy are faultless in terms of adherence to the Bible and patristic dogma, the words of the American prayer book (in the context of lack of clear doctrinal teaching in the Episcopal Church) can easily be taken to mean that the One Person of God, with three Names, has an everlasting kingdom. Often these days in that Church the three Names are made non-sexist—Creator, Redeemer, Sanctifier. It would have been far better had the original Greek Blessing been used without any editing and simply as the words of the celebrant. Once we try to simplify we take on a task that is far more complex than most of us either realise or recognize.

In the volume of *Initiation Services* the Church of England has followed the lead of the Episcopal Church in the use of these words but has modified the punctuation possibly to make them less likely to be taken as an expression of the doctrine that God is One Person with Three Names. Thus on several occasions these lines appear at the beginning of a service:

Blessed be God, Father, Son and Holy Spirit.
Blessed be his kingdom, now and for ever. Amen.[1]

Again, why could not the original blessing from the Orthodox Liturgy be used? for it is not only, after all, the original, but is also doctrinally clear, verbally attractive and not open to the charge of Modalism.

Finally, we may note the "act of faith" in the "Ministry at the time of death" in the *Pastoral Services* which is as follows:

Holy God,
Father, Son, and Holy Spirit,
I trust you,
I believe in you,
I love you.[2]

Again, an orthodox mind can state this and mean the God as set forth in orthodoxy but at the same time its common-sense meaning seems to be that of telling a God with three Names that you trust, believe and love him as one Person, which is Unitarianism.

With respect to the identity, role and work of Jesus of Nazareth, that which we refer to as Christology, we have already noted that his being pushed out of the Psalter is a most serious loss to Christian

1 pp. 103, 122,134,143 and 154   2 p. 223

worship, for it decreases its Christ-centredness. Further, we have already raised questions in discussing the Nicene Creed concerning the advisability of the translations, "eternally begotten of the Father" and "of one Being with the Father" rather than "begotten of the Father before all worlds/ages" and "of one substance with the Father". Here we raise further questions about the way in which Jesus Christ is presented in different parts of *Common Worship*.

One of the innovations of *Common Worship* is that an authorized Affirmation of Faith may be used instead of a Catholic Creed. One such is the poem/hymn, specially written by Bishop Timothy Dudley-Smith, which begins, "We believe in God the Father".[1] Poetry is a wonderful medium for expressing certain thoughts and feelings but it is hardly appropriate for expressing the dogma of the Church, which needs precision in propositional statement. This weakness is well illustrated in these lines:

> We believe in Christ the Saviour,
> Son of God in human frame,
> virgin-born, the child of Mary
> upon whom the Spirit came.

In the original Nicene Creed, there is an accumulation of phrases to state the precise relation of the Son to the Father and of the "descent" of the Son in Incarnation into the world, in and through the womb of Mary, the virgin. Here the content of the Nicene Creed (or the Apostles' Creed, or both) is simplified so much that the words can support error and heresy. "Son of God in human frame" does not (for a church Creed) adequately convey the nature of the Incarnation, that the only-begotten Son of the Father took to himself in the womb of the Virgin a full and complete human nature and made it his very own so that he is One Person made known in Two natures, divine and human. "In human frame" hardly communicates the assumption of a total human nature, body and mind/soul. It is not even clear whether the Spirit is declared to come upon Mary or upon the Son of God or both. The lines "virgin-born ... " and "upon whom ... " can be read as stating that when Jesus was born the Spirit of God descended upon him and thereby God the Father adopted him as his Son, the Son destined to be his Messiah and Saviour. Presumably they are intended to teach that Jesus was born of Mary, the virgin, and that her conception of Jesus was caused by the direct action of the Holy Spirit, but one can only claim this if one already is familiar with the classic formulations of the Church in her authoritative Creeds.

The simplifying or carelessness in the expression of the classic dogma of the Person of Christ is seen in various collects and post-communions. The Post-Communion for Christmas Day runs:

1 p. 146

God our Father,
whose Word has come among us
in the Holy Child of Bethlehem:
may the light of faith illumine our hearts
and shine in our words and deeds;
through him who is Christ the Lord.

The theological problem here is the way in which the Incarnation of the Word or Logos or Son[1] is presented. The use of prepositions in theology and collects is often critical for the conveying of what becomes accurate or inaccurate meaning. Here "in" is a bad choice for it suggests that the Son is contained in the baby Jesus as the yolk of an egg is contained in the shell. What theology has called "the hypostatic union", that there is one Divine Person who is made known in two natures without any confusion, is hardly presented here. Rather it seems that this prayer joins Charles Wesley who erroneously (but attractively) wrote, "Veiled in flesh the Godhead see", in his well known hymn, "Hark the Herald Angels Sing".

In the Collect for the First Sunday of Christmas the petition to God the Father is, "grant that, as he [the Son] came to share our humanity, / so we may share the life of his divinity." Again, the desire to simplify as much as possible has made something near to, if not, heresy. Certainly the eternal Son and Logos/Word took to himself and made his very own our human nature, which he received from the Blessed Virgin Mary. Certainly in spiritual union with him in the Body of Christ and by the action of the Holy Ghost, we partake of everlasting life, which comes to us as pure gift from the Father and the Son by the Holy Ghost. Yet it is not a matter of simple equivalency, that he shares our humanity and we share his divinity, as this Collect suggests. We can never be as he is—One Person with two natures, human and divine. We are each a single human being with only a human nature which by grace can be, as the Orthodox say, divinised and deified by the presence in it of the Holy Ghost.

The Post-Communion for "The Naming and Circumcision of Jesus" seems to have not rightly understood the Christological hymn in Philippians 2:5–11 where the humiliation and then the exaltation of Christ is described and celebrated. The hymn ends with his being given the Name above all names, the Name revealed to Moses at the burning bush, YHWH, the LORD. Yet we read:

Eternal God,
whose incarnate Son was given the Name of Saviour:
grant that we who have shared
in this sacrament of our salvation

1 See John 1:1–12.

> may live out our years in the power
>   of the Name that is above all other names,
> Jesus Christ our Lord.[1]

First we have "the Name of Saviour" and then the title of "Jesus Christ our Lord" but there is no clarity as to what is the Name above all other names. Who would guess from this prayer that the Name is YHWH, LORD? Perhaps the confusion is caused by seeking to use Philippians 2 in a context where it is not directly applicable. There was no need in the final part of this Prayer to introduce "the Name that is above every name" (verse 9).

Having taken examples from the beginning of the Christian Year let us now turn to the end. The Post-Communion for The Last Sunday after Trinity (Bible Sunday!) tells "the God of all grace" that his Son Jesus Christ "fed the hungry with the bread of his life and the word of his kingdom." Then it requests that he sustain his people "by your true and living bread". Certainly Jesus, the Son, preached the Gospel or word of the kingdom and certainly according to John 6 he feeds people not only with material bread but with the bread that comes down from heaven, the bread of everlasting life. But to state that he fed the hungry "with the bread of his life" by the lakeside is to be in danger of losing the distinction between on the one hand the unique life of God, wholly possessed by the Father and the Son, the gift of everlasting life from the Father and the Son, which enters into human nature to sanctify it and immortalize it, and on the other ordinary bread as food.

Finally, a few more examples of carelessness or inaccuracy in statements of the doctrine of the Incarnation of our Lord. From the "Common of the Saints" here are the opening lines of the Collect for The Blessed Virgin Mary:

> Almighty and everlasting God,
> who stooped to raise fallen humanity
> through the child-bearing of blessed Mary ... .

Certainly the Blessed Virgin is the *Theotokos*, the birth-giver of God the Son in his assumed human nature, the Infant, Jesus. Certainly also Mary's cooperation with the God of Israel was absolutely necessary to make the Incarnation of the Son possible. But, it is to exaggerate or to be imprecise to state that God raised fallen humanity by her child-bearing, for two reasons. First, God the Father raised fallen humanity in Christ to the heights of heaven through the total mission and saving work of the Son of God, not through Mary's child-bearing; and secondly, "child-bearing" is a general expression and thus can refer to Mary's having had other children as well as Jesus (which many Protestants believe that she did).

---

1 *Common Worship*, p. 427

In the "Seasonal Provisions"[1] of Eucharistic Prefaces there are all kinds of expressions concerning the Incarnation which belong more to the ornately sentimental than to the plainly accurate. Yet there is one expression, left over from the translation of the Nicene Creed favoured in *The Alternative Service Book 1980* but discarded in *Common Worship*, that is retained. It is "by the power of the Holy Spirit" with reference to the conception of Jesus by Mary. The 1980 translation was: "by the power of the Holy Spirit he became incarnate of the Virgin Mary" (in contrast to the *Prayer Book* rendering of "was incarnate by the Holy Ghost of the Virgin Mary"). Objections were made to the 1980 rendering on the ground that (a) there is no basis in the Greek or the Latin originals for "the power of"; and (b) theologically all of us are conceived by the power of the Holy Ghost, for he energizes the act of procreation in the natural world, but the conception of Jesus was made unique, by the immediate personal presence of the Third Person of the Holy Trinity. However, the expression "by the power of" appears in several of these prefaces. For example, "was born of the Virgin Mary by the power of your Spirit"[2] and "Mary ... conceived by the power of your Holy Spirit."[3] The first of these is careless, suggesting that her giving birth rather than her conception was the time when the Holy Spirit was especially present and the second is inaccurate for she conceived "by the Holy Ghost" personally as the Nicene Creed teaches on the basis of Luke's Gospel (1:35 where "Power of the Highest" is a Name of God).

In *Pastoral Services* there are several examples of carelessness in the stating of Christology. In "Thanksgiving for the Gift of a Child" it is stated in the Introduction: "God became one of us in Jesus, and understands all that surrounds the arrival and upbringing of children ... ."[4] This is not a true statement. The only-begotten Son of the Father took to himself in the Virgin's womb our human nature and made it is his very own. God did not become one of us in Jesus but the Son of God Incarnate is named Jesus.

It is not often recognized that there are Christological (as well as devotional) implications in changes to the Calendar. Take the period of fifty days from Easter to Pentecost which, for over a thousand years in the West, and still so in the *Prayer Book*, included Easter Day, five Sundays *after* Easter, Ascension Day, the Sunday after Ascension and then Whit Sunday. Here the Feast of the Ascension is given the importance that, as a Festival of the Lord Jesus, it rightly deserves. There are forty days before it and ten days after it, following the biblical, chronological presentation in Acts 1 and 2. In *Common Worship*, beginning with Easter Day (which is called The

1 pp. 300ff.   2 p. 303   3 p. 311   4 p. 202

First Sunday *of* Easter) there are six other Sundays *of* Easter before the Feast of Pentecost. Here the attempt of the modern liturgists is to recover the period of "the great Fifty Days" of the third-century Church before the Feast of the Ascension gained prominence and entered the Calendar. The general effect of this piece of restoration of an ancient arrangement in a new context is that the Feast of the Ascension, and thus the doctrine of the Exaltation of the Lord Jesus, can be and is neglected, downplayed or ignored. Further, to add insult to injury, congregations are often taught that the public confession of sins in these fifty days is not appropriate because it is a period of celebration, which should not include penitence. (We have noted that in genuine biblical piety the true confession of sin is also the real praise of God, who is celebrated as just and merciful.)

It is perhaps worth observing that the results of the fixation of liturgists of the last third of the twentieth century on "the early Church", and their attempts to put primitive patterns into modern worship to replace that which originated in the medieval period, are with us in all kinds of ways, with the most obvious being the general walkabout and greeting called "the passing of the peace" at the centre of the Eucharist. We can only speculate as to what liturgy would have looked like today had there been in the general culture and in the churches of the 1960s and 1970s (a) a deeper appreciation of the medieval centuries and what the Church achieved by the grace of God then, and (b) little or no fascination with the vaguely primitive and early as having a certain superiority to the later developed forms. Whatever "the Peace" actually was in the third and fourth centuries (and who really knows?) it developed in such a way that the Church abandoned that form of it. Thus it ceased to be a period of congregational movement and encounter and become a simple, quiet and dignified act between priest and people.

Conclusion

The simple point we are making is that modern liturgy should be as accurate as ancient liturgy when it comes to being faithful to Scripture as this Scripture was understood and given dogmatic expression by the Early Church and confirmed by the reformed Churches of the sixteenth centuries. Oversimplifying or dumbing down or sentimentalising are not appropriate when expressing the central, holy dogma of Mother Church. Further, when the results of simplifying occur in the Daily Office, its constant repetition causes imperfect and imprecise understanding of the basic dogma of the Church in some of her most devoted members, who pray daily in a structured way. We hear often the claim that "the law of praying is the law of believing." By this principle, claimed as coming from the Early Church, modern liturgists are able to change the doctrine of the Church. That is, they write their modern services in which there may be (unwittingly or deliberately) imprecision, vagueness or error in the expression of classic dogma. When the services are approved by a church synod their content is said to be what we are to believe on the basis of this "law". In the Episcopal Church of the USA, this was given deliberate form in the new Catechism of the new Prayer Book, authorized in 1979. The committee which produced the Catechism did so by studying the new rites approved for this prayer book and by use of the inductive method produced the doctrine set forth in the Catechism, "An Outline of Faith", of the Episcopal Church. Apparently no account was taken either of the classic Formularies of the Anglican Way or of the Rite 1 traditional texts in this enterprise. Thus the doctrines of God, Christ and Man within it do not obviously agree with the statement of these doctrines in the Formularies and in the dogma of the First Four Ecumenical Councils of the Church.

Happily, as yet no Catechism has been produced from the abundance of new material in the volumes of *Common Worship*. However, if the law of praying is the law of believing, we are in great danger. It is possible, as has been done in brief here, to go through the newer compositions of Liturgies, Litanies, Collects and Post-Communions and to show that some of them lack precision, or are even in clear error, in their presentation of such basic doctrines as theology proper (God), Christology, pneumatology, anthropology and soteriology. Again it seems that the quest for relevancy and intelligibility, that has so influenced the Church since the 1960s, has led to cutting corners and taking short cuts in linguistic expression. The result is often not the greater intelligibility that was the aim but, at best, vagueness. Sadly, one must also raise the possibility that this situation may also reflect the educational background of the writers who probably are not so well tutored in patristic and classic theology as were their forefathers, and this despite their preference for models from the Early Church.

CHAPTER TEN

Thou and You[1]

In *Patterns for Worship* (1989) the Church of England Liturgical Commission provided guidelines to those who were writing their own local liturgy. Included in the nine points were these two: "Address God as you" and "Use language that includes women as well as men."[2] It appears that in all the advice offered in the last decade by the experts to worship leaders in parishes, there is none that says, "It is quite all right to address God as 'Thou'" and "Women are included in traditional English."

A little of the total provision that is *Common Worship* is in the traditional language of prayer and worship—e. g., the Services of Holy Communion Order 1 and 2 in Traditional Language. In contrast, most of *Common Worship* is in what is called "contemporary language", which both involves addressing the Deity as "You" and striving for gender inclusiveness so that feminists feel that they are included in the services. So, for example, instead of "brethren" we have "brothers and sisters" and instead of "the man" we have "the one" or "they". This modern search for inclusiveness is in stark contrast to *The Book of Common Prayer* (1662), the King James Version of the Bible and the hymns of Charles Wesley and Isaac Watts, wherein the Deity is most clearly the "Thou-God" and the language is (by modern criteria) patriarchal, androcentric and sexist, even as it is also judged to be in the original Hebrew, Aramaic, Greek and Latin of the Bible and the early Liturgies of the Church. However, it is most important to note that *Common Worship* has not yet gone as far down the road of gender inclusiveness as have other modern prayer books. The Holy Trinity and the Three Persons thereof are still named in the biblical, patristic and orthodox way as the Father, the Son and the Holy Spirit and the pronoun "he" is used of the Godhead and the Persons thereof. In other parts of the

1 This chapter makes use of Peter Toon and Louis R. Tarsitano, *Neither Archaic nor Obsolete*, 2003, to which the reader is referred for a fuller discussion.
2 *Patterns for Worship*, p. 273

Anglican Communion, especially America and New Zealand, gender inclusiveness is being developed and applied as much to deity as to humanity!

Revolution in the 1960s

When did the change in the addressing and naming of God occur? It seems clear that it began in the 1960s, gained momentum in the 1970s, has continued to roll since then and shows no sign of stopping in the new millennium. The 1960s was a time of social and cultural revolution in the Western world, especially in America. It was during this revolutionary period, and as an aspect of it, that all the mainstream churches of the English-speaking world, in their accommodation to the changing culture and Zeitgeist, began their move from addressing the Lord God as "Thou" to speaking to him as "You". One can be reasonably sure that it was a cultural phenomenon, rather than a theological development, because it was not only the old Protestant Churches (e. g., Lutheran, Presbyterian, Anglican and Congregationalist) but the new Protestant Churches (e. g. Assemblies of God, Southern Baptists and Church of the Nazarene) who participated; and even more amazingly it was not only Protestants but also Roman Catholics, who far outnumbered any Protestant denomination in the USA, who joined in. This was a phenomenon that knew no denominational, sectarian or kith-and-kin boundaries.

With little preparation, and sometimes with unbridled enthusiasm, millions of Christians, tutored by preachers in white suits and clergy in black robes or bright vestments, dropped the traditional, long-standing English language of prayer that they had been using (alone or alongside Latin) in public worship. They replaced it with a contemporary form of English, taken from the secular idiom of the time, a language that—as was soon demonstrated—would be always open to adjustment and development, as society and culture changed. They read the Bible, said prayers, ministered sacraments, preached sermons and gave blessings in this new language that was called "contemporary" English to distinguish it from "traditional" English as found in the King James Version of the Bible, *The Book of Common Prayer* and their old hymnbooks. And in doing so they were told by their ministers that by making their services of worship more intelligible and simple, more accessible and relevant, more down to earth and less élite, they would attract and hold the young people (who in the 1960s and 1970s were apt to reject the old institutions of public life) and at the same time not drive away the older folks. And, together with the paradigmatic change in speaking to God, there came all kinds of further changes in what was said about him (or her), and done for him (or her), as well as in the music used to celebrate what was proclaimed as his/her enabling and affirming presence.

It will be recalled that in the late 1920s the Church of England prepared a revised edition of *The Book of Common Prayer* (1662) which was eventually not approved by Parliament because of its supposed "Romish" trends. However, the language, idiom and dialect of prayer were wholly in the very same traditional language as the *Prayer Book* of 1662 that it was intended to replace, and nobody at that time in Church, Parliament or general population in the British Empire thought this to be odd or wrong. Then, even after World War II and the social changes it caused, the Anglican Church of Canada published its revised version of the *Prayer Book* of 1662 in 1960/62 and once again this was wholly in the traditional language of prayer, with apparently no pressure for modern language, even though some of its content was affected by "the liturgical movement", then gaining influence. Further, when in mid 1960s the process of "liturgical renewal" officially began in the Church of England, the first set of trial texts called Series 1 & 2, with their new structures or shapes and content, still used traditional language to address God.

Only in 1966 was the decision taken in the Liturgical Commission to begin to look into the possibility of producing modern language services. Thus in 1967 the Liturgical Commission published *Modern Liturgical Texts* and a year later the international Lambeth Conference of Anglican Bishops gave the green light to the use of contemporary language for God in the worldwide Anglican Communion of Churches, even as the Lambeth Conference ten years earlier had given the green light to liturgical revision (including departures from the structure and content of the classic *Prayer Book*). Alongside this dramatic change in Liturgy, and perhaps prior to it, a similar change was occurring in the translation of the Bible as new versions were being planned and produced to meet contemporary needs. So it came to be that the new "You-God" was encountered in both sacred Scripture and holy Liturgy, including new hymns and choruses.

It is well known that a living language does not change overnight but evolves slowly. Yet here, in English-speaking churches in the 1960s and 1970s, without any previous development and adaptation of language to draw upon, and no tried and tested models to follow, a dramatic and major change was achieved. There had been no trial runs to test the market, as it were—even though a few hymns and choruses had been around for a while addressing God as "You" or using "Thank you Lord" in a chorus. The revolution was quickly and efficiently executed, as if driven by an irresistible force. It was a change that involved no natural evolution. It was planned and decreed from the top but was not opposed over much at the bottom, except for pockets of resistance such as those who formed societies for the defence of the *Prayer Book* and the *King James Version* of the Bible (the American Society for the Preservation of the Book of Common Prayer was formed in 1971 by academics who could see the trend and where it was going). The rapid move from the so-called "traditional" to the so-called "contemporary" is therefore more likely to be explained meaningfully in terms of religious, social and cultural factors rather than by the normal evolution of language. Many people were simply swept along by it without consciously saying "yes" to it. There was no public discussion followed by a referendum. The powerful cultural winds blew and kept on blowing and what they caused to happen just stayed there, albeit in an unstable form, ever searching for further development and expression.

To take one important case. Why did Evangelicals generally enthusiastically embrace the revolution? It appears that many evangelical Christians in America and Britain were taken up with the themes of relevance, intelligibility, accessibility and simplicity. They wanted to have a simple message from an accessible Bible using intelligible forms of services in plain person's speech in order to evangelise their fellow citizens, especially the youth, and bring them into "a relationship" with the Saviour, Jesus Christ the Lord. They believed that the "traditional language" with its mystery and poetic quality was not, and could not ever be, effective to this end with the type of people who had inherited or caught the spirit of the 1960s. Modern people in a modern world dressing in modern clothing and using modern technology needed to hear a vibrant, modern message in a language that was much the same as they used and heard day by day. In short, it was believed that God the Father and the Lord Jesus Christ would only become really and convincingly available, accessible and intelligible to the majority, if these divine Persons, together with the Holy Spirit, were addressed as "You". To keep on using "Thou, Thee, Thy and Thine" with strange verb endings for God was to put people off and thus to miss a great opportunity to offer the gospel of the revolutionary Jesus Christ to a people who craved for the "New".

Reasons offered by scholars and church leaders for totally new translations of the Bible (such as the *New International Version*, "the Evangelical Bible", the *New English Bible*, the *Revised English Bible*), and for replacements for the *King James* (or *Authorized*) *Version*, the *Revised Version* and the *Revised Standard Version* (such as the *New Revised Standard Version*), included the availability of better manuscripts of the Greek New Testament, better knowledge of the Hebrew text of the Jewish Bible, the presence of archaic words in the old versions to be replaced, and that no distinction was made in the original Hebrew

or Greek between addressing God and a human being in terms of the
pronouns and verb forms used. But at the street level the reason given
for new versions and paraphrases was quite simple. The *King James
Version* was not understood and modern language versions were needed
to open the Bible to ordinary folk, young and old. Young Protestant
ministers were taught in their colleges that they could not trust the
KJV for it was not an accurate translation of the originals; they
needed a modern, contemporary and accurate version from which to
preach to a generation of young people who were rejecting the old
ways. Further, young Anglican clergy were taught that *The Book of
Common Prayer* was not based upon the best texts of the Bible in the
original languages or the best understanding of the worship and
doctrine of the Early Church. Moreover, it was supposedly written in
a nearly inaccessible Tudor English and its content was too much
concerned with painting human beings as "miserable sinners". They
needed not only an accurate but also a modern Prayer Book for
leading the people in public prayer and genuine Celebration.

Many of the consequent innovations were presented as
experimental. Whatever the genuine attractions of the reasoning
behind them, forty years later we are in a better position to see that,
in England at least, the experiments have missed their aim of
bringing Christianity to ordinary people and the young.

At the same time, thousands of Roman Catholic parishes had
begun using "contemporary" English for their Masses and the
Roman Church was being shaken from top to bottom as it embraced
aggiornamento (up-dating) and *reaccentramento* (re-centring). The
decision by the Roman Catholic Church in the late 1960s to go from
the Latin into the vernacular and to have one form of English for the
whole and vast English-speaking world was taken in the Vatican in
Rome. It was assumed that a basic English could be utilised that was
intelligible and accessible to English-speaking Catholics wherever
they lived, be it in North America, Australasia, the West Indies,
Africa, the Philippines, India and so on. The resulting English Mass
was in a form and style that no-one spoke, that was lacking any sense
of mystery and transcendence, and that was only contemporary in
the sense that it was not traditional. From those days to the present,
there has been strong agitation within the Roman Church for
improvement of the English as well as for a return to the use of Latin
in some situations. And there is evidence that there is now a
sympathetic ear in the Vatican City.

Underneath the call for relevance, intelligibility, accessibility and
simplicity and the claims that better scholarship was being used for
Bible translation and liturgical revision were other reasons, the
underground springs that supplied the streams and lakes. These were

the ideas and ideologies that made the 1960s into a period of major discontent, change and revolution in the western world and in America in particular. All who lived in this period, even if cloistered in the Vatican, or drinking sherry in an English country rectory, or teaching in Oxbridge, breathed into their souls some of this new air and ferment. In fact, even those who rebelled against the innovations and changes of the time were affected by them, so powerful was this Zeitgeist! Having breathed in this new air and having been blown by this new wind, church leaders (without necessarily consciously thinking it through) felt impelled to introduce the new, be it a new language for worship, new forms of service, new designs for churches, new seating arrangements within them, new hymns, new music, new dress for clergy, new emphases for the agenda, a new ethos—a new gospel. It seemed at times that the 1960s had discovered and made available to the 1970s a new God, a God who was much more intelligible, accessible, available, plausible, believable, warm-hearted, friendly and less judgemental than the transcendent God of the 1950s and of traditional Christianity. In fact, in the 1960s he had been brought down from on high to be present within the "community of faith". He had to be given a new name, the "You-God" and the name of the former God, the "Thou-God", had to be used as little as possible—better, not at all.

Returning to what was happening in the Church of England, we may recall that Series 3 was the name given to a series of new trial services, addressing God as "You", produced by the Liturgical Commission in the late 1960s and early 1970s. In introducing them the Commission wrote:

> The change from *thou* to *you* when praying to God will be difficult for some people; but we must be careful to look at the problem in its true perspective. By a linguistic accident, the *thou*-form, which was a highly intimate mode of address in Cranmer's day, has become generally obsolete; but through its survival in prayers it has acquired a sacral tone which the Reformers did not intend.[1]

Most clergy apparently accepted this argument with little or no serious questioning, even though it is not a sound argument. They also accepted without much hesitation the (doubtful) argument presented by the translators of the new versions of the Bible—e. g., the *New English Bible*, *Jerusalem Bible* and *New International Version*—that there is nothing in the originals of the Bible to justify the use of different pronouns for God and man in modern English, since in Hebrew and Greek the same pronouns are used for both.

1 *Commentary on Holy Communion Series 3*, 1973, p. 7

The Revolution Examined

So what people were told and what many of them came to believe
from the 1970s in the English-speaking world went something like
this: "There is absolutely no need any longer to address God with the
archaic, second-person-singular pronoun (*thou, thee* with *thy & thine*
and the old verb endings). It was right to use *thou* in the sixteenth and
seventeenth centuries; but it is not right to do so today because we
do not use this pronoun any more in contemporary English. We should
use the same pronoun to God as we do to man, for to do so is to speak
naturally and normally. In fact, in this usage we are being true to the
spirit of the sixteenth-century Reformers who spoke and wrote in the
idiom of their day. Further, the Bible in its original languages supports
us in doing so for there the same pronouns are used of both God and
man. God was not set apart for special linguistic treatment!"

We need to show why such claims are at least partly false, and why
at the same time there are good reasons why intelligent people
should have the opportunity to use in its fullness the official language
of prayer of the Church of England.

We can all agree firstly that in the main languages used in the Bible
and in the Church of East and West up to the sixteenth century there
are two different second person pronouns, one for the singular and
one for the plural. It is also true that the Lord God and Jesus Christ are
addressed by the same pronoun as a man—second person singular.
Thus in the rendering of the original texts into English in the sixteenth
century the translators used the singular "thou/thee/thy/thine" of
both God and one man/woman and used the plural "you/ye/your" of
more than one person. They also followed the same rule in the
rendering of medieval liturgical texts into English, as Archbishop
Cranmer's translation and editing of the Collects amply demonstrates.
Not surprisingly in 1611 the translators who created the *Authorized
Version* of the Bible kept to this plan as they found it in the English
Prayer Book and English Bibles of the sixteenth century.

In the second place we need to be aware that, while the second
person singular ("thou") was widely used in the sixteenth century in
everyday speech, the (grammatically speaking) second person plural
("you") was already used to one person in certain contexts, and used
so regularly that *not* to use it would have been as extraordinary as for
us to address a king as "thou". This distinction is even found in the
1662 *Prayer Book* and also, from 1549 onwards, in the Ordinal now
usually included in copies of the *Prayer Book*. In the Catechism the
catechumen is addressed both as "you" and "thou", to distinguish
different relations to the Church and thus to God the Father—"you"

when he is viewed as being a Christian through the faith of his godparents acting on his behalf, and "thou" when he has embraced the faith for himself and stands in an immediate and intimate relation to God, the Father, as a believer.

The use of a second *singular* "you" in the "Form of Consecrating a Bishop" is even more informative. As the Archbishop delivers a Bible to the newly ordained bishop he addresses him to begin with, as we might expect, using the words *thyself, thou* and *thee*. Then, perhaps surprisingly, he switches to *ye* and *you*. "Be so merciful, that ye be not too remiss; so minister discipline, that you forget not mercy … ." This is not because there is suddenly more than one bishop. With both "thou" and "you" one man is being addressed, and "you" is used just as we would use it, as a singular.

In each of the eight questions put to the bishop-elect, as well as in the introduction and final statement of the questioning, the Archbishop similarly addresses him as "you" and "ye". "Are you persuaded … ?", "Will you maintain … ?" and so on. Now in the parallel questions addressed to the candidates in the other two ordination services, of deacons and of priests, "you" is also used, but only when it is assumed that several men are being ordained together and so the plural is required. Nowhere in these two services is an individual man addressed as "you". So why are bishops treated differently? The explanation is not far to seek. In making these distinctions the Reformers were indeed using the language of their age—in which the normal address to God in the second person singular was already sharply distinct from the common speech of address to our earthly superiors. In the sixteenth century "thou" was the form of address in an intimate relation or to a social inferior, while "you" was already the *only* polite form of address to the great ones of the earth, the only variety being some odd uses of the *third* person: "Will your majesty dine?" and so on. There, the possessive pronoun is unmistakeably the second plural used to one person. Since a bishop was a lord spiritual, he was properly addressed as a temporal lord or a king would have been, in the plural. However, in divine worship he is a servant of God and like everyone else can be "thou". This politeness of plural address was never extended to God.

Thus the word "thou" to God was already special in the sixteenth century and *did* have a sacral tone from the very beginning of liturgy in English. By the beginning of the seventeenth century the "thou" form was becoming obsolete among educated people in common conversation. It was regarded as a rustic form and used for addressing inferiors or even as a deliberately contemptuous form of humiliation; and it was retained by some poets. On the other hand the second singular was still unchallenged as the form of address to God.

From the seventeenth century onwards, then, "you" became the most used form in English for addressing one or more human beings and "thou" was increasingly used only to God. In *A Short English Grammar* (1753), written for the children in the Methodist Kingswood School, Bristol, John Wesley, the great communicator and evangelist, stated this principle most clearly as ordinary grammar: "We say 'Thou, Thee' to God and 'You' to man." And this rule was used by his brother, Charles, in his 4,000-plus hymns. It was also the rule followed by virtually all educated English-speaking people from the seventeenth century to the 1960s. So for a long time when "thou" was unheard in common educated non-religious speech, no other pronoun was used to God.[1] The distinct, sacral language of prayer flourished and developed for four hundred years.

If asked why they addressed God as "Thou" and not as "You" in public worship, family devotions, metrical psalms, hymns and spiritual songs, people in the eighteenth, nineteenth or twentieth centuries gave reasons such as these: (a) its sacral tone communicates both a sense of apartness from God who is wholly different from us and a sense of intimacy with God who comes near to us in Christ Jesus by the Holy Ghost; (b) its being grammatically singular not plural underlines and upholds the Christian doctrine that God is One God, even though a Trinity of Persons (and that to call God "You" raises the possibility [yet not necessity] of Tritheism with God becoming a plurality not a unity); and (c) its long, deep and wide history as the focal point of the English tradition of prayer keeps the church of today in the full stream of English worship and devotion and preserves continuity of faith and worship.

With the experience of thirty or so years of "contemporary language" in church services, we can now demonstrate by simple comparisons that Liturgies and Directories (from various denominational sources) which use "Thou" generally have a stronger sense of human sin, of God's holiness, of the absolute centrality of the saving work of Jesus Christ, and of the comfort of the Gospel, than those which use "You". In fact "You" liturgies seem to belong to a different level, even type, of Christian doctrine as they usually claim to be celebratory, in contrast to what their users call the sombre and penitential nature of the "Thou" forms. Further, it is obvious to many of us that the "You" address to God not only has the effect of detaching us from our past (to which we surely belong in the communion of saints) but has also quickly adapted itself since the 1970s to the secular demands of society, as the continuing attempts by the churches to be inclusive and not gender-specific in their

---

1 "Thou/thee" continues to be used for addressing human beings in certain rural and urban dialects in the twenty-first century; but the use is obsolete in standard English speech.

contemporary language of prayer well demonstrate. Without doubt we may say that the "You" idiom is in a state of flux and, as yet, no seemingly permanent form of it has been worked out.

In fact, as we have observed, not until the 1960s did any sizeable group of people even begin to think that the long-standing English language of public prayer was not appropriate for people who felt themselves to be totally modern. As well as those who had an evangelistic passion "to reach the unsaved" and saw the use of ordinary street language as a great advantage in communication, the "You" address to God was welcomed by those caught up in the revolutionary decades of the 1960s and 1970s. They felt that the change in pronoun brought God nearer to the people of a democratic and egalitarian world, with its emphasis upon human and civil rights and familiar relationships. They believed that a God to whom they could talk as to a fellow traveller better fitted where they were in the great search for up-to-date-ness (*aggiornamento*), relevancy, and meaningfulness in life.

Finally, we may note that the resistance to addressing the Lord God as "You" came from the minority (a) who were less caught up in the *Zeitgeist*; (b) who placed a high value on the inherited tradition of the language and literature of public prayer; (c) who strongly felt that there is a real and important—even necessary—sacral tone in the "Thou" address to God; (d) who believed that the communication of biblically orthodox doctrine in and for worship is almost inextricably tied to that form and idiom used and perfected over the centuries; (e) who held that the "You" form could not easily or quickly become a language of prayer if the qualities of reverence and intimacy, biblical orthodoxy and traditional devotion/piety were to be prominent, and (f) who challenged the assumptions of the liturgists that the only proper liturgical language is that of the man/woman in the street; and that language is no more than a means of communication, with no emotional, affective and numinous role. They felt that by insisting on the most commonplace language in worship the modern liturgists were making it difficult for people to have a sense of the wonder, mystery, majesty and glory of the eternal and infinite God.

Language and Style

Let us now move on to note why intelligent and informed people, including not a few distinguished writers and teachers of prose and poetry, have stated in varying degrees of intensity since the 1970s that modern liturgies, versions of the Bible and hymns for public worship have no style. It will be appreciated that this is a larger concern than merely criticising a change from "Thou" to "You" in addressing God in public prayer. Let us presume in charity that they possibly know what they are talking about, that there is a possibility that they are at least in part right, and that we want to know precisely what it is they are saying and claiming. Further, let us confine ourselves specifically to Liturgy to keep the discussion manageable.

First of all, we need to clear the ground and explain what it is they are not saying when they say that there was no style in the contemporary rites printed in such books as *The Prayer Book* (1979) of the Episcopal Church, USA, *The Alternative Service Book 1980* of the Church of England, *The Book of Alternative Services* (1985) of the Anglican Church of Canada, and the Church of England *Common Worship* (2000). They are not saying that the Liturgical Commissions produced necessarily bad or illiterate prose or that these services are not in some ways educated and careful compositions. Further, they are not claiming that those who produced them had bad intentions such as desiring to undermine the Christian religion or drive people from churches. And they are not saying that some of these services are totally unattractive or without meaning to some people, especially those who feel that the church must move with the times. What they are saying is that these modern liturgies have no distinctive features of language specifically appropriate for their unique purpose as services of worship, because those distinctive and required features are not available in the modern world that gave them birth. They are also convinced that there is nothing to distinguish the language of modern liturgical rites from that of a piece of secular writing, except that technical words from the Bible and theology (e. g., grace and glory) and phrases from the old liturgy ("communion of saints") are used by them, and that some pomposity of rhythm is occasionally attempted.

To make this point clearer and explain their case more carefully, we need to make use of several technical terms. We are all aware that our language can be used in a whole variety of ways and in differing contexts and circumstances. This is referred to as *register*, which may be defined as "a variety of language as used by a particular speaker or writer in a particular context". And when a number or group of people, who share a common interest or purpose, use the same *register* in a reasonably consistent way, *register* becomes *style*. Here *style* is not something to be praised or blamed as such for it is a descriptive not an evaluative way of speaking.

There are many examples of *style* in English—e. g., that used for debates in the British House of Commons, for addressing judge and jury in courts of law, for the composing of pop songs, for the working of computers, for describing American football, and so on. The form of language in each of these examples is clearly recognizable as belonging to a specific context and usually serves little or no purpose outside that context.

Is there a *style* for public worship in English that is recognizable? Yes there is and it is that found in *The Book of Common Prayer*, the *King James Version* of the Bible and in classic English hymnody (Watts, Wesley, Keble etc.). Certainly this *style* was much better known in 1960, but it is still known and recognized today. People who are not regular churchgoers recognize this *style* immediately when, for example, the traditional forms of the Ten Commandments or the Lord's Prayer or the Apostles' Creed or "Thus saith the Lord" are quoted. If people hear, "And with thy spirit," most recognize religious language, but this is hardly the case if they hear its modern form "And also with you". This point also applies in the use of phrases ("world without end"), clauses ("hallowed be thy Name") and sentences (e. g., "Those whom God has joined together let no man put asunder").

The central point that the critics of modern liturgies have made is that there is no religious *style* available in written and spoken contemporary English. That is, there are no appropriate *registers* to communicate certain basic feelings and convictions—e. g., for awe and reverence towards superiors, for earnest petition of what we cannot demand as a right, and for love which we know we are unworthy to express except by permission of the beloved. Social structures and family relations have changed and contemporary language has necessarily changed with changes in society and culture (and thus modern language is disposed towards the democratic, egalitarian and utilitarian). However, the absolute need for certain forms of expression, relatedness and address in the public language of worship has not changed because of the need to communicate certain givens (e. g., concerning the nature and character of God and the situation and need of man) that are there in the basic Revelation to which the Holy Scriptures witness and of which the Liturgy speaks and sings.

The critics think that the creators of modern liturgical texts had a most difficult and probably impossible task, for they sought to produce in a modern form of language a style that the language itself could not in its late twentieth-century or early twenty-first century modern forms fully deliver or allow. The reason for this is that it does not contain a *register* of what may be called the basics of a modern religious language that can communicate at one and the same time reverence and contrition before a transcendent, holy God and genuine intimacy with him in communion, fellowship and friendship through his grace. Sometimes half-aware of this, modern liturgists have sought to make use of the traditional language of prayer (e. g., the verb, "Grant ... "); but language wrenched from its original context and placed in an unfamiliar context shows that it is not working by sounding and feeling odd.

So (the critics conclude) it has in reason to be accepted that only one genuine religious *style* is available, and that this traditional language of prayer and worship has the real potential to put people in the right mood and disposition for reverence and attention before God and for intimate communion with God (if he graciously makes this possible). It alone has the potential and wherewithal (as God allows) to make possible the subtle and varied relation of the worshipper to the Holy Trinity, who is Creator, Redeemer and Judge. While modern forms of English, using theological terms, may take pilgrims some of the way towards worshipping the LORD God in spirit and in truth and in the beauty of holiness, only the genuine *style* of traditional language of public prayer can do the work really well (again as God graciously permits). The fact that the traditional language/style of prayer was fashioned in Tudor English and then used everywhere by all until the 1960s is, for devout Christians, part of the providence of God that they gladly accept.

Conclusion

We may regret that the slow and solid development of the English idiom and classic language of prayer was virtually stopped short in the 1960s. Had it not been so we do not know what could have been—e. g., in the writing of new hymns to express Christian Faith in the conditions of the late twentieth or early twenty-first century. Further, we do not know what solid improvements there could have been made to *The Book of Common Prayer* (1662) if Liturgical Commissions had actually lived within and sought to think within the received English language and style of common prayer.

What is not usually recognized is the significance of the fact that the Formularies of the Church of England—*Prayer Book*, Articles and Ordinal—are themselves written in the traditional idiom of the language of prayer and doctrine. Therefore, even as these Formularies stand as more authoritative than any form of alternative services and statements of faith (even those in *Common Worship*), so the classic, traditional language stands before the modern attempts to create a new language for public worship and translation of the Bible. Therefore the official language of public prayer of the National Church remains that found in the *Prayer Book* and the *King James Version* of the Bible. In saying this it needs also to be admitted that since at least the seventeenth century the sermon and notices were given in the modern form where "you" serves for both singular and plural when human beings are addressed outside the liturgy and its Bible readings. However, what is absolutely clear is that the authentic English language of public prayer addresses God as "Thou" not "You", and in providing the guideline, cited above, "Address God as you," the Liturgical Commission was exceeding its authority and giving bad advice.

Bearing this is mind, it is probably unwise in public worship to mix the two different languages of prayer, the so called "traditional" and "contemporary". The traditional has been around for a very long time, possesses a logic of its own, and has acquired a style in which meaning is associated with particular forms of words and expressions. In contrast, the new one is still searching for an identity and its own logic and style. The two do not mix well, even at all, even as oil and water do not mix. It would therefore seem to be the case that it was a major mistake to include in *Common Worship* actual texts from *The Book of Common Prayer* even if these texts are adapted and modified and thus not precisely the same as their originals. They are, however, of the same shape and with nearly identical ingredients. As used within the general provisions of *Common Worship* and alongside a Psalter, Bible and Prayers that are most likely to be in contemporary language, the logic of language and the internal consistency and style of the traditional language is broken. And there is the further point, which has been made elsewhere, that if *The Book of Common Prayer* is the standard against which the doctrine of *Common Worship* is to be judged, that permanent standard should not be part of the temporary usage.

Epilogue

It would be foolish to underestimate the challenge being faced by the Church of England as a national and established Church situated in a secular culture which has deeply penetrated individuals and society as a whole. Though a majority of citizens of Great Britain state on their Census form that they are Christians, their expression of that religious preference is rarely through public worship, except at Christmas and at weddings and funerals. More often it is in private forms and ways. Thus the question of how to attract people to the regular public worship of God in the Name of Jesus Christ in such a nation is not easy to solve, especially when the Church has chosen to replace the ancient forms of service provided in *The Book of Common Prayer* with a major modern Directory of options for services. Once the tried and the familiar, with minimal choice, is set aside and replaced by the multiple choice of a kind of religious supermarket, one real problem becomes what to choose from the seemingly endless possibilities and permutations.

The General Synod of the Church of England has moved, from the position of presenting to the nation the possibility of either worship according to the *Prayer Book* or according to the limited choices within *The Alternative Service Book 1980*, to offering to the nation from 2000 one vast collection of outlines and ingredients for services under the general title of *Common Worship* and including the primary services of the *Prayer Book* within this collection. And it has done so while paying lip service to the authority of the *Prayer Book* of 1662 as a primary Formulary of the Church. Let it be clear that Synod has not attempted to ban the *Prayer Book*, which only the Parliament could do; but, it has sent out the message, if only in sign language, that parishes no longer really need the *Prayer Book* even if they intend to use its provisions, since its major content is located within the main volume of *Common Worship*. This noted, one needs also to state that it is generally agreed in the General Synod that, in the Church of England as a whole, the attitude towards *The Book of Common Prayer* (1662) is considerably more favourable than it was in 1980 when, by all accounts, overtly hostile attitudes towards the *Prayer Book* were far from uncommon. Further, if Synod had the power to ban the *Prayer Book*, such a move would be overwhelmingly rejected now (which it might not have been a couple of decades ago). But the position of the *Prayer Book* has changed. In 2003 *The Book of Common Prayer* is regarded only as one small though essential ingredient of the "smorgasbord" that is the liturgy of the modern Church.

So we find in 2003 that the Liturgical Commission on behalf of the General Synod has produced for the Church of England a vast liturgical provision or Directory called *Common Worship*, and alongside it has produced explanatory essays and books, which local worship leaders are encouraged to study before planning local services. Despite its great bulk, the production of the corpus is a task that is not yet ended since texts already produced have a restricted life and have to be revised and new ones (e. g., on initiation) have to be designed and produced. In comparison, the provision within *The Alternative Service Book 1980* was, despite its weaknesses in doctrine and style, a much smaller, restricted, unified and somewhat simple alternative to the *Prayer Book*.

In a task so vast, taken on by a national Church seeking to be comprehensive, open to the winds of change blowing through society, and attempting to attract people with privatised religion back to public worship, the probability of making mistakes, and getting important as well as minor things wrong, is great. So anyone of a sound mind and sensitive disposition, who buys the various volumes and takes the time carefully and sympathetically to review rationally and calmly the basic design and contents of the enterprise, soon realises that parts of this collection are strange, wrong or misguided. It is as if the Synod and Commission were engaged in a task that began to define them rather than they it and so they did not know when to stop (and still do not seem to know as the publication of *Additional Collects* in 2003 shows). There is apparently a satisfaction for the liturgist in the constant planning, creating and getting approved, and a related satisfaction for much of the Synod in vetting and approving this or that new service, set of prayers, or advice on how to put together a suitable public service of worship.

The most obvious thing wrong with the whole thing is the title. To call the whole by the adjective "Common" is to enter into a basic redefinition of the word and call something the very opposite of its true nature. "Common" in religious usage has for centuries pointed to the specific liturgy of *The Book of Common Prayer*, a liturgy which has a fixed structure and content and thus presents very little scope for innovation locally, except in the addition of hymns and ceremonial. The effect of this vast provision of *Common Worship* with its many options is certainly not to produce a common way, structure and content of public worship at the parish level throughout the two provinces of the Church of England. It is rather to create a situation where each parish does what is pleasing in its own estimation and judgement, believing that it is being "led by the Spirit" as its "worship leaders" meet regularly to plan the public services for the next Lord's Day, choosing a shape and ingredients from the possibilities provided. Innovation and change rather than tradition and stability are the names of the game. Thus parishes a few miles apart geographically may be a million miles apart liturgically in terms of the form and contents of worship as well as in the idiom of prayer used. If they notice this and begin to ask probing questions, it will be told them by Rural Dean, Archdeacon or Bishop that if they are getting the shape/structure of the service right and are putting into it only approved ingredients (supplied in the volumes of *Common Worship*) then they will truly be making it possible for people to worship God in a modern, dynamic way.

Another serious problem that is noticed in reviewing the texts is that the preferred language of the Synod and Liturgical Commission, the idiom known as "contemporary liturgical language", is not a stable language. Rather, it is a changing language as it both seeks to retain traditional words, expressions and syntax from the old texts and also absorbs certain ways of speech and prohibitions from the secular agenda of the world. Even within the texts produced by the Commission and approved by Synod over the last decade one can see changes made in the language. On the one hand, the liturgists are more conscious of the demands of, say, the feminist movement in 2003 than they were in 1999 and, on the other, at the same time, they want to bring on board those whose piety is still rooted in the idiom of the old *Prayer Book*. Thus, even as linguistic changes have been made in 2000 to the texts approved in 1980, so it is highly likely that much of the material in the present texts will be judged inappropriate in ten years' time, simply because what is deemed acceptable in terms both of speaking of human beings and of describing and addressing God will have changed.

Further, one cannot help noticing that, within the multiple ingredients in the variety of options that are provided in contemporary language for *Common Worship*, there are examples of imprecision in the statements of the central dogmas of the Faith, of disagreement with the theology of the classic Formularies, of poor translation of original texts, of misuse or misunderstanding of biblical texts and sources, of overplaying the "social gospel", of diminishing the significance of sin and the crucial importance of personal salvation, of unsuitable phrases and images in prayers, of unutterable prayers, of excessive simplifying or dumbing down, of failure to make anything memorable, of not producing a sense of the numinous, of being too related to the "horizontal" and too little to the "transcendent" dimension of grace, and of slack phrasing and syntax. Then, also, it is not surprising that, as the whole thing grows in size, doctrine or instruction in one volume contradicts that in another.

Then, we must not avoid facing the serious question as to whether the power to invent our own services for public worship is good for us as scholars in the school of Christ Jesus. We need to ask: Does the "perfect freedom" of his service mean the same as the freedom of supermarket shopping? however restrictive our choices may seem to others? Making up our own services according to our own tastes can be a way of avoiding spiritual discipline and the painful aspects of sanctification. Rather than facing the regular demand to conform ourselves to the Word of God and to be shaped by the Holy Ghost according to the doctrine and discipline of the Church, the constant choice—by the few entrusted to do so—of content and ingredients replaces the idea of an ascetic rule with one of personal preference. It is a typical vision of modern life: specific and hard-edged content is replaced by technique or a common "structure". However, without the fixed content, the shape, with the variable ingredients, can become a vain form. This kind of "Common Worship" makes self-expression more important than formation in godly habits and holiness. The intercessions become "prayers of the people", the peace enforces sentimental cosiness, and making sure that as many people as possible get a public role in the "main Sunday service" is viewed as more important than having things done well. The theological implications of making the priest (already construed as the President) into a Master of Ceremonies seem not to be considered. This changed understanding of worship and sanctification may be a bigger challenge to classical Common Prayer and all that it entails than the actual content of the "Common Worship multiplex".

It appears to be the case that in 2003 many ordinary members of the Church of England are blissfully unaware of the whole story and provisions of *Common Worship*. They may be aware of the main volume which some churches have placed in the pews, but more likely they have their services for Sundays, Baptisms, Weddings and Funerals printed in a booklet and so do not see any of the several volumes. In fact, it appears to be widely believed amongst the laity that *Common Worship* is simply the most recent form of a modern language alternative to the *Prayer Book*, replacing the book they were recently told to send for (reverent) recycling, which they called "the ASB". They change their car every five years or so and thus they are not too surprised to see their modern liturgy changing every twenty years. However, as they do not change their old Georgian or Victorian house for a modern purpose-built mobile home, so they do not expect *The Book of Common Prayer* to disappear from the bookshelves at the back of the church, and they are upset when it is taken away by impetuous clergy. Most of the faithful are not yet aware of the massive effort of bishops, liturgists and some clergy during the last decade to broaden the meaning of "common prayer" so that the ancient book of that name is merely one optional element in the totality of possible options and permutations. In fact they do not yet grasp fully the fact that a revolution has occurred in their church. Sooner or later they will catch up with the news.

A calm consideration of the situation suggests that the Church of England has embarked upon a path leading to a goal which will eventually be utter confusion of identity, style and commonality. The flood gates of choice have been opened and the pressure of the waters, energized by the Zeitgeist, is pushing them open even wider. Good people will grow increasingly weary as they have to choose continually what to include in their Sunday worship or as they have to endure the results of that choice. Those outside the churches who could be attracted to enter them will be turned off by the inability of the Church of England, as a National Church, to present a coherent message and form of worship for the nation. People everywhere, including the young, will become confused, upset and angry because deep down in their souls they yearn for solidity, stability and excellence in public worship. It seems probable that *Common Worship* will eventually collapse under its own weight and volume, even if every incumbent and lay leader has it all on the hard drive of his computer as well as on CDs. The vast provision takes so much time and preparation to consider carefully, and does so when time is precious, since the work load of the clergy and lay leaders of the Church of England is getting heavier, not lighter, as patterns of ministry are radically changed to face economic and pastoral reality. What *is* there to say except that the situation is a real mess and will get worse because the continuous manufacture of new "worship material" is not improving it!

So it is hardly surprising that groups of dedicated churchmen are rejecting the path of *Common Worship*. Probably five hundred parishes, maybe more, that are linked to the Forward in Faith movement, and that are Anglo-Catholic in doctrine and worship, have already voted with their feet, as it were. They conform their practice to that of the Church of Rome and use the Missal, Sacramentary and Breviary of that Church, even though many in their number recognize the poor quality of the English idiom used in these texts. Then there is another minority voice firmly yet gently saying that there is nothing wrong with the ideal of common prayer, that is, with the post-sixteenth-century tradition of forms of worship uniform throughout a large Church, which system served both the Church of England and the Church of Rome well for many years. One of the most important virtues of *The Book of Common Prayer* is having all the necessary elements for worship bound together in a single volume that is the common possession of clergy and people. As soon as one begins to approach the "smorgasbord" of liturgical options that *Common Worship* provides the balance is inappropriately tipped in favour of the "designer" whether the clergy or a local committee including the lay insiders. Better to have one book, the *Prayer Book*, and submit to the discipline of learning its devotional logic and inviting others to join in this spiritually energizing exercise.

Those who have decided or will decide to stand with *The Book of Common Prayer*, to use it and to promote its use, and not to encourage the use of *Common Worship*, will act well within the spirit and the law of the land and of the Church. Not only should they seek to make their use of the services of the *Prayer Book* reverent and attractive to those who are genuinely searching for meaning—for God—in their lives, but they should also seek to do much alongside the use of, and in harmony with, the *Prayer Book* to encourage people to leave their privatised religion, join in the truly Common Prayer and experience the fellowship of the Household of God. There is obviously opportunity to use modern means of communication through web sites, video and sound cassettes to CDs to promote classical worship that is different in ethos and content to what is provided by way of entertainment and edification in the world around. And, of course, the way is wide open to offer an apologetic for and instruction in the godly life to which the *Prayer Book*, using the Bible, calls us.

Then there is some mileage in exploring the need for supplementary forms of worship that cater for modern situations not envisaged by *The Book of Common Prayer* (1662). For example, there is a need for some kind of children's liturgy (specifically for children, rather than for "family" or "all-age" services attended by adults for their own benefit, as well as by children). This could be a simplified act of worship including such elements as the Lord's Prayer, the Apostles' Creed, the short (and in some cases long) form of the Commandments and the Collect of the Day in their *Prayer Book* forms and words, with appropriate teaching and some special children's prayers composed in the same idiom as used in the *Prayer Book*. This would help to dispel the totally unfounded assumption that children's services cannot and should not be done with traditional texts in the classical English language of public prayer.

After all, we know that in England thousands of children go several times each week after school to mosque, synagogue and temple to learn prayers and texts in Arabic, Hebrew and Punjabi! Yet another area for exploration is the revival of the writing of hymns in the classic idiom of public prayer and providing a hymnbook for use with the *Prayer Book* that is wholly supportive of it.

Although many will seek to live in both worlds, that of Common Prayer and "Common Worship", perhaps the best way forward is not to mix these two but to see *Common Worship* for what it is, an alternative to but not replacement of, the real *Common Prayer*. Thus parishes are to be encouraged to choose which of these ways to follow, the original or the innovative, in order to bring a consistency of theory and practice to the parish life. *Common Prayer* is by its nature jealous of its position and does not sit happily with competitors. When it is not followed according to its own internal rules it ceases to be what it is, a total provision, in well tried and stable ways, for a whole nation, a whole parish, a complete family and a baptized believer of a godly life through the worship of God.

To conclude. *Common Worship*, despite the scale of its innovations, its concern with Shape and its pastoral sensitivities, is not truly a viable alternative to *The Book of Common Prayer*. It has too many volumes, in which are too many rites and options, not a few of which are of mediocre quality as spoken English. It is imaginatively impoverished by the dominance of the single image of "a journey", and, finally, as we have shown, *Common Worship* is of doubtful orthodoxy as Christian liturgy.